In this account of his journeys a[...] Le Donne provides a set of personal and thoughtful reflections on what is at stake in the theological, historical, and social relationships among Christians and Jews. Through anecdotes, snippets of conversation, and interaction with the work of Jewish and Christian scholars, Le Donne addresses such sensitive issues as the "war on Christmas," the Holocaust, dogma, anti-Judaism and anti-semitism, and more optimistic topics such as laughter and love, belief and belonging. Le Donne shows courage by facing directly difficult questions such as the Christian role in paving the way for the Holocaust. Throughout, he shows not only respect for Jews and Judaism but tremendous understanding of Jews in the twenty-first century. He recognizes, for example, that Jewish identity does not depend on religion, faith, or observance. The book is highly readable and engaging, and will be of interest to anyone interested in a down-to-earth and honest approach to Jewish-Christian relations.

—ADELE REINHARTZ, PROFESSOR, CLASSICS AND
RELIGIOUS STUDIES, UNIVERSITY OF OTTAWA

This extraordinary book is Jewish-Christian dialogue at its very finest. Professor Le Donne lives out what he teaches. As a Christian, he learns about God, forgiveness, faith, and love from his Jewish friends, and the wisdom he gains is to be treasured. In his allowing his friends to ask him the most difficult questions, he shows the heart of a seeker for truth—ultimately the heart of a teacher on fire for divine friendship made concrete in love of neighbor.

—MATTHEW LEVERING, JAMES N. AND MARY D. PERRY JR.
CHAIR OF THEOLOGY, MUNDELEIN SEMINARY

Writing from the borderlines of Christianity and Judaism, Le Donne offers a sympathetic, accessible, and openhearted reflection on the relationship between faith and lived reality. This book is a thoughtful, humorous, and honest response to how we should we live in the presence of neighbors and friends who are both like and unlike us. The Jewish-Christian encounters that Le Donne experiences have served to strengthen his faith; similarly, this book will both educate and enrich the reader.

—DR. ED KESSLER, WOOLF INSTITUTE, CAMBRIDGE, UK

Argument with Judaism has featured perennially—sometimes violently—in Christianity. Anthony Le Donne explores the stubborn facts of that conflict by means of a wideranging and reflective discussion of the cultural faultlines that have driven human communities apart. Taking his analysis into his personal experience, he shows that living with an awareness of the culture we live in can redeem us from the sin of oppressing others and stunting our own faith.

—BRUCE CHILTON, BERNARD IDDINGS BELL
PROFESSOR OF RELIGION, BARD COLLEGE

Near
Christianity

Near Christianity

How Journeys along Jewish-Christian
Borders Saved My Faith in God

Anthony Le Donne

ZONDERVAN

Near Christianity
Copyright © 2016 by Anthony Le Donne

This title is also available as a Zondervan ebook.

Requests for information should be addressed to:
Zondervan, *3900 Sparks Dr. SE, Grand Rapids, Michigan 49546*

Library of Congress Cataloging-in-Publication Data

Names: Le Donne, Anthony, 1975- author.
Title: Near Christianity : how journeys along Jewish-Christian borders saved my
     faith in God / Anthony Le Donne.
Description: Grand Rapids : Zondervan, 2016. | Includes bibliographical references.
Identifiers: LCCN 2016022156 | ISBN 9780310522966 (softcover)
Subjects: LCSH: Christianity and other religions--Judaism. |
     Judaism--Relations--Christianity.
Classification: LCC BM535 .L3483 2016 | DDC 261.2/6--dc23 LC record available at
     https://lccn.loc.gov/2016022156

Cover design: Brian Bobel
Cover photo: iStockphoto.com
Interior design: Denise Froehlich

Printed in the United States of America

---

16 17 18 19 20 DHV 10 9 8 7 6 5 4 3 2 1

For my mother, Patricia,
who first taught me about books.

HAPPY BIRTHDAY, MOM.

Contents

Foreword

In her introduction to *The Misunderstood Jew*, Amy-Jill Levine presents these recollections in an autobiographical mode: "When I was a child, my ambition was to be pope. . . . I was raised in North Dartmouth, Massachusetts, a suburb of New Bedford, in a neighborhood that was predominantly Roman Catholic and Portuguese. Thus my introduction to the church was through ethnic Catholicism, and it was marvelous: feast days and festivals, pageantry and mystery, food and more food. . . . When I was seven, this early fascination with Christianity came to a head with two events. First, I became insistent upon making my First Communion. . . . Second, that year a friend on the school bus said to me, 'You killed our Lord.' 'I did not,' I responded with some indignation. . . . 'Yes you did,' the girl insisted. 'Our priest said so.'"

I was born about a decade earlier than A.J. and 550 miles to the south, in Richmond, Virginia. I remember there being a Baptist or Methodist church on nearly every corner. None of them was more prestigious than the First Baptist Church, located at the very spot where Monument Avenue and the Boulevard met. Facing an equestrian statue of Robert E. Lee and sharing the beauty and history of the neighborhood with the Virginia Historical Society, the Daughters of the Confederacy, and the Virginia Museum of Fine Arts, this was where Richmond's movers and shakers congregated every Sunday.

I don't remember having any close school friends who attended this church or any of the other Christian congregations in town. And I don't recall that I was much concerned about it one way or the other.

All of my good friends, from grade school through high school, were Jewish. But not just that: they were members of Beth El, Richmond's conservative synagogue, most of whose families—like mine—were from Eastern Europe. What went on at Beth Ahabah, the Reform congregation with a large German Jewish contingent, was as foreign to me as the services at First Baptist Church.

Therefore, for better or worse, I lack any of the colorful first-person stories that A.J. amassed. More than that, I can't remember anyone accusing me of being a Christ killer or baiting me by calling me a Jew, dirty or otherwise. The only time I can recall my religion being a factor was when the president of the University of Richmond, the Southern Baptist institution I attended as an undergraduate, referred to me as a "fine Christian gentleman." I was certain then—and remain steadfast in this view today—that he intended this comment as a high compliment.

Without, I hope, overstating or undervaluing the importance of the life each individual lives (our autobiographies), I firmly believe that what we've seen, done, and experienced, whom we've met, how we were treated, where we lived—and countless other details—go a long way toward defining who we are, what we value, and how we interact with others. This is as true for scholars as for anyone else. It is, I affirm, not by chance that we study what we study, teach what we teach, and structure the evaluations that we promote or deride.

For quite some time, scholars tended to be reticent about introducing themselves into their work. When "complete objectivity"—a chimeral goal if ever there was one—was held in highest academic esteem, it made some sense, I suppose, to reduce, if not eradicate, the "I" of the writer. I don't know many people today who tout the virtues or even possibilities of completely objective scholarship. Perhaps from a robot, but probably not even from such a source would we expect or appreciate a mechanistic or values-free exposition of religious belief and practice. This is not to say, of course, that anyone is free to misrepresent, but everyone is entitled to an informed perspective, the product of what that individual experienced, learned, imagined, and constructed.

The work that follows this foreword is Anthony Le Donne's—as are the words. It is his story, and he tells it magnificently. Allow me to highlight three of its most salient characteristics. First are its authenticity and honesty. Although I cannot vouch as a first-hand witness for any of his autobiographic narratives, I do not doubt that he has recorded them all exactly as he recollects them. This ring of truth is a consistent feature of Le Donne's account of his experiences, his beliefs, his doubts, and his many interactions with others as individuals or within a group.

Second, this book is informative. All readers, myself definitely included, will learn a lot—about their own faith, the faith of others, and the journey we all set out on. I suspect that each reader will feel, at some point or other, as if Anthony has captured just what they have been thinking or doing. And such readers will also acknowledge how much richer a picture they now have of other faith communities and their adherents.

Third, but by no means least important, this work is entertaining. Clearly, there are serious sections, where a light touch is not appropriate. But readers will respond to other sections with smiles and chuckles (even the occasional guffaw!). Anthony knows how to tell a story. The opening pages of chapter 6 are, word for word, one of the funniest stories I have ever heard (or read). And what's more, Anthony's analysis of this autobiographical tale succeeds in enhancing its humor and expanding our understanding of humor in general.

I have two further observations, admittedly of a more personal nature. I will pose them as questions. First, how do I, as a non-Christian, relate to this work? I should add that I am primarily a scholar of the Bible and of Judaism, not without some knowledge of Christian texts and history. In instances where he touches on these matters, Anthony basically reaffirms much of what I have learned from decades of studying and teaching.

But I don't actually know that much about lived Christianity—how Christians apply their faith in specific circumstances and under particular conditions. Here Anthony excels. If I may say so, his is an authentically lived Christian faith—not the only way to be a Christian, of course, but an authentic way. His dedication to a Christian life joins all of his narratives and all of his analyses. This is what a Christian does, this is how he does it, and this is why. Again, I hasten to acknowledge my understanding that this is not the only way.

This emphasis on Christian faith in action, if I may use such a term, also richly informs Anthony's interactions with texts, including the many passages from C. S. Lewis that he cites. His inclusion of texts is not an intellectual adornment to parade his erudition before awed readers. Rather, he brings these texts and their authors to life, so that real conversations emerge—among Anthony, his readers, and the many authors he brings in. And the result of such conversation is the thoughtful articulation of paths (often diverse paths) consistent with an equally thoughtful Christian life.

And, second, how do I as a Jew—a Jewish scholar and scholar of Judaism—evaluate Anthony's portrayal of Jews and Judaism? Short answer: it is excellent. I see myself in many of the encounters Anthony has with Jewish colleagues, and I see my colleagues in others of his encounters. Let me quickly add, because it does bear repetition even for those who know it well, that Judaism is not a dogmatic religion and that historically and traditionally Jews value the free and open exchange of ideas, ideas that often lead to distinct and distinctive practices.

That said, I observe that Anthony's book is not a comprehensive introduction to Jews and Judaism, nor is it intended to serve such a function. Rather, it chronicles the many times Anthony has fruitfully engaged Jews in conversation—with what might appear to be a rather unexpected result: what Anthony learns about Judaism leads him to rethink some basic beliefs and practices within Christianity. And, as a result, this introduction, or better reintroduction, of Judaism into Christianity enhances and deepens his faith. What a marvelous notion! Even better because in Anthony's skilled hands it does indeed work.

Do I, as a Jew, have any concerns at all about Anthony's procedures or judgments? Not really, but sometimes I get the impression that he thinks more of us Jews than we rightly deserve. There are indeed some brilliant Jews, there are for sure deeply spiritual Jews, and there are Jews who authentically apply Judaism's basic tenets to every facet of their lives.

But we can also be a rowdy, even raucous bunch, difficult to characterize, impossible to organize. I wouldn't have it any other way. Nor do I think that Anthony wishes to make any major changes in his Jewish colleagues, as individuals or as a group. When we exist collaboratively and cooperatively, as with Anthony and his Jewish friends, then do we fulfill to its fullest the vision that the biblical prophets bequeathed us. May God grant us the perception and patience to acknowledge this.

—LEONARD J. GREENSPOON, *Klutznick Chair in Jewish Civilization, Professor of Classical and Near Eastern Studies and of Theology, Creighton University*

Introduction

Mere is always a dangerous word.

—C. S. LEWIS, *THE FOUR LOVES*

The title of this book is a play on C. S. Lewis's celebrated apologetic, *Mere Christianity*. This is not a book about Lewis. Rather it is about how Christianity comes into better focus and in higher definition when we compare notes with our closest neighbors. I tell this story from the perspective of a Christian who has roots in and sympathizes with evangelical Christianity. I will leave it to my readers to determine how evangelical I am. I imagine that some will find this question debatable. Even so, evangelical is my native religious language. It is because of my native fluency that I have included a C. S. Lewis–themed subplot in this book.

Lewis, whom I have come to admire anew in recent years, had a notion to distill Christianity to its "thinnest" elements. He meant to capture the essence of the faith. Lewis attempted to "explain and defend the belief that has been common to nearly all Christians at all times." He did this, he believed, in service to his "unbelieving neighbours."[1] Lewis's portrait of *mere* Christianity has stood the test of time as a compelling view from the inside.[2] This book, *Near Christianity*, occupies a different vantage point by asking, What does Christianity look like from the borders?

In asking this question, my project differs in scope and intention from *Mere Christianity*. Rather than focusing on Christianity's distilled essence, I will examine ancient, storied, tragic, and often misunderstood borders—the complicated and shifting borders shared by Jews and Christians. We can learn much about ourselves by examining our center, but we also learn much and perhaps much more from our boundary markers. I have selected a handful of vantage points along Jewish-Christian borderlands, including pilgrimage, the "war" on Christmas, and mass murder. In each case, I intend to complicate and expand rather than distill and narrow. I offer no simple morals for Christian living or belief. Relationships are complicated. Life is complicated. I see little virtue in reducing or oversimplifying problems that require complex discussions.

When we Christians talk about Christianity—especially when we think outsiders might be listening—we tend to talk about essential Christian beliefs or the ideals shared by almost all Christians: our idealized center. Sometimes we point to the teachings of Jesus or Paul and describe their visions for a new, improved community of faith. This way of getting at Christianity is not necessarily faulty. Understanding a people's highest aspirations provides a window into who they are (or want to be). Lewis's masterwork is a model of this method. What an apologetic like *Mere Christianity* will not tell you is what Christians take for granted, what motivates them, and what they are really like in the real world. A different path of self-reflection is required if we are interested in the borders rather than the beliefs of Christianity. In my experience—in my conversations with "unbelieving neighbours"—I have learned that Christianity appears quite differently from the borders.

Take, for example, the so-called war on Christmas. Unlikely to be found in a systematic theology textbook, it is an important border issue: many Jews experience Christmas differently than many Christians. I find this difference interesting and I am not certain that anyone has the right idea for a way forward. More important, I think that this topic—which seems to be peripheral to Christian theology—might reveal something at the very heart of Christianity. Or consider the theological importance of humor. I never would have thought to write chapter 6 had I not seen a national survey of American Jews who were asked to define their Jewishness. After realizing how crucial a "good sense of humor" is for Jewish self-definition, I began to see

> In my experience—in my conversations with "unbelieving neighbours"—I have learned that Christianity appears quite differently from the borders.

my own Christian relationships differently. Humor is not a topic addressed in any Christian creed or seminary faith statement. Yet it is essential to my experience as a Christian. Most of the chapters in this book take a peripheral topic and suggest that it may be more important than I previously thought.

Also different from Lewis's classic, this book is not written for my "unbelieving neighbours." Rather this book is for my fellow Christians. I do not doubt that my Jewish friends (and other neighbors) might be listening to this internal conversation. Even so, this book is not an apologetic for perceived outsiders. I would not feel qualified to write that sort of book. Even if I did, improving upon a classic is almost always a losing proposition.

This book is not a response to any particular book by Lewis. I do—perhaps too often—nod appreciatively to Lewis in these pages. My evangelical roots allow me to feel the depth of his influence. Furthermore, my own moral and intellectual development has rendered me less conservative on the topics of Scripture, the afterlife, Jesus' epistemological limits, and Scotch whisky. On these points I suppose that I have evolved (or transgressed) toward Lewis's less conservative tendencies. The flip side of the coin is that I part ways with Lewis's theology at times.

Lewis's *Manqué* Commentary

Noteworthy for my topic is Lewis's inadequate and limited view of Judaism. Lewis used the word *manqué* to describe Jews. The "unconverted Jew" seemed to him as "someone very carefully prepared for a certain destiny and then missing it."[3] In my view Lewis's narrow scope limits him severely on this subject. So while *Near Christianity* is not a book-length answer to C. S. Lewis, I should from the start address this particularly important topic relating to our neighbors.

No doubt, we are creatures of circumstance, and Lewis's closest contact with Judaism was in his friend, lover, and wife, Joy Davidman. Thus Lewis had an inclination to extol the virtues of Joy's status as a "converted Jew." He writes of this most directly in his foreword to her book, *Smoke on the Mountain: An Interpretation of the Ten Commandments*:

> Another point of interest in Joy Davidman's work comes from her race. In a sense the converted Jew is the only normal human being in the world. To him [*sic*], in the first instance, the promises were made, and he has availed himself of them. He calls Abraham his father by hereditary right as well as by divine courtesy. He has taken the whole syllabus in order, as it was set; eaten the dinner according to the menu. Everyone else is, from one point of view, a special case, dealt with under emergency regulations. . . . We christened gentiles are after all the graft, the wild vine, possessing "joys not promised to our birth"; though perhaps we do not think of this so often as we might.[4]

Davidman, as Lewis explains, was from "the second generation of unbelief; her parents, Jewish in blood, 'rationalists' by conviction." Lewis favorably related her turn from atheism to his own conversion. Both Davidman and Lewis had experienced life at a critical distance from Christianity only to be converted later in life.[5] Lewis was predisposed by theology and personal affection to see Jews and Judaism as incomplete until brought within the circle of Christian faith.

My own contact with Jews and Judaism is much different and much less intimate. At the risk of oversimplifying a complex relationship, you could say that Joy Davidman met Lewis within the confines of a shared faith. Certainly many borders were negotiated to make such a meeting possible. This is not the sort of meeting that most Jews have in mind. Many would see Davidman's embrace of Christianity to be a departure from her Judaism.[6] I seek no similar conversion from my Jewish friends. As I read the Bible, I find that God has made promises to his first love (mysteriously, so it seems, according to Romans 11) and that this God is not inclined to forget promises.

I realize that my view is not the standard Christian view. Lewis's *manqué* commentary probably represents the thinking of many more Christians, living and dead. But Christians have a long history of misunderstanding Jews and Judaism. In many cases we have defined Judaism as something very similar to Christianity but lacking in the key element of Christ. In doing so, we set ourselves as the ideal and begin our measurements of "them" with observations of what they lack. Lewis did not invent this misperception, but he does echo it.

Lewis spent years "near" Christianity in angst. His conversion was a war of attrition and one that he was glad to concede in the end. Lewis took a step toward his completed self as he was won over by Christ. It is understandable that he would see those beyond the Christian border as incomplete. But this has not been my experience of Jews who reside near Christianity.

To judge outsiders by the standards of insiders is in my opinion something other than gracious. It is a transgression that St. Paul (to whom Lewis alludes in his vine metaphor) adamantly opposes. Paul, a Jew of the first century, believed that non-Jews had a different relationship to Jewish standards as they were communicated in Scripture. According to Paul, to use these standards to measure the status of neighbors was a misuse of Scripture.

But it will not do to treat Lewis too harshly. In none of his writings do I find the sort of Christian who says, "I am saved and you are not," or, "I am in the good graces of heaven and you are not." Lewis knew well that he was flawed and that Christianity is populated by flawed people.

Lewis spent years "near" Christianity in angst. His conversion was a war of attrition and one that he was glad to concede in the end. Lewis took a step toward his completed self as he was won over by Christ.

He takes a much different tone when he discusses the ideals of faith than he does when discussing the practicalities of faith. Consider these words written in his *Reflections on the Psalms:* "I am inclined to think a Christian would be wise to avoid, where he [sic] decently can, any meeting with people who are bullies, lascivious, cruel, dishonest, spiteful, and so forth. Not because we are 'too good' for them. In a sense because we are not good enough. We are not good enough to cope with all the temptations, nor clever enough to cope with all the problems, which an evening spent in such society produces."[7]

Lewis knew well that Christians are a flawed people. We are both much more and much less than our ideals. We are a messy people who act in unsystematic ways. There is only so much that a well-communicated system of belief will reveal about us. "The problem is not simple and the answer is not going to be simple either."[8]

Finally—perhaps most important—Lewis knew that Christianity was more than the *mere* image he provided in any single book. The Christian life is complicated, varied, and inconsistent. (I think that Lewis has this in common with Paul.) My point is simply this: a Christian on the borders is a different creature, and Christianity as lived out in the real world cannot be reduced to key Christian ideals. The fortified citadel of belief is a form of Christianity, no doubt. But Christianity is also the mess that spills out to the unfenced borderlands. We are more likely to meet our neighbors in the mess of real life than in the ivory tower of apologetics.

Conversation, Not Apologetics

So much of apologetics derives from an assumption that Christianity makes sense. This assumption is not necessarily foundational, prescriptive, or systematic, but it is common. The apologist invites you to "think it through." Implicit here is a promise: if you just think about Christian theology long enough, clearly enough, and with the right mental tools, it will all make sense. And the parts that fail to make sense would indeed make sense if only you had more time, clarity, and the right mental tools to figure it out.

While I have no doubt that some Jews think this way too about Judaism, this is not my experience of Jews and Judaism. After my intentional proximity to Jews and Judaism, I am more inclined to ask, Why should I expect any of this God-talk to make sense? I am grateful when I happen to wrap my mind around a theological topic. But I am surprised every time I do. Reducing God within the confines of human language should always be an uncomfortable business.

I teach seminarians. So I am a strong advocate for thinking it through, for clarity of thought, and for using the right mental tools. Even if (especially if) I am doing everything right, shouldn't I expect my view of God to become ever more complex? The more I learn of how God works or does not work in the world, the less adequate I should feel putting words to it—the less confident I will feel in my adequacy.

Acknowledging such complexity also reveals the problem with asking, What do Jews believe about X? or, What does Judaism teach about Y? This is a very Christian way to approach interreligious dialogue. Moreover, we often feel frustrated by the complexity

> The more I learn of how God works or does not work in the world, the less adequate I should feel putting words to it—the less confident I will feel in my adequacy.

it takes to explain that (1) there is nothing that unifies Jews except Jewishness, and (2) Jewishness is variously defined. But why shouldn't this be the case? If God is endlessly complex, shouldn't we expect God's children to reflect this complexity? And if God is highly particular, unified, and distinct, shouldn't we expect God's children to reflect this too?

This book is not about what every Christian does or should believe about God, God's people, or God's world. I will not be able to tell you what Jews believe about these matters either. I can only explain my experience of Jewish-Christian borders. I will attempt this with the hope that I can explain something that I believe to be true about Christians and Christianity. Even so, I will confess my own inadequacy. No matter how well my own story touches the larger history of Jewish-Christian relations, my attempt to make sense of my experience will inevitably fail on a few levels. My experience of Jewish-Christian borders is only mine, and I do not believe objectivity is possible. For my part, I have tried to be honest and self-aware. I am certain that this book will not be nearly enough to satisfy the topic.

Lesson Number One

Perhaps the first and best lesson I have learned about Jewish-Christian dialogue is that the Christian walking into the conversation looking for simple answers will be frustrated. But sometimes the Christian who displays some acknowledgment of Jewish complexity might be met by a straightforward and simple answer. Philosopher Ted Cohen points to an important difference between Jewish conversation/study and Christian doctrine/apologetics. In Jewish talmudic study, the logical possibilities are often valued over decisive conclusions.

> It is the essence of this tradition that these debates, these arguments—let us call it "this study"—goes on and on. Of course resolutions are found, consensus develops, and not everyone's opinion is of equal weight. But there is no systematic finality. . . . A person in this tradition does not only learn and memorize the conclusions reached, although he must do some of that. Rather, he joins this study: He argues, debates, contests, criticizes, and learns; and he does not stop.[9]

Cohen then points to a Jewish asymmetry with Catholics: "In a word, there is no Pope."[10] Or, reframed for evangelicals, there is no systematic finality to defend, no C. S. Lewis.

This book offers no final doctrinal statement at the end of each chapter. I have resisted hard and fast concluding statements wherever possible. I hope that the chapters herein suggest bigger and wider conversations.

Jews Are Not Judaism

You will find that I often use the two-sided phrase "Jews and Judaism." For example, in my discussion of anti-Semitism I write that Christian worship services regularly refer to "Jews and Judaism." I am very aware that this is a cumbersome way to write. It is, however, necessary: Jews are not Judaism.

The "ism" of Judaism suggests a unified belief system or way of being in the world. When exploring the "ism" of this historic faith, we can observe a number of interesting differences between Judaism and Christianity. For example, Christianity is deeply invested in the idea of original sin, whereas most Judaism is not. Or we might notice that Judaism has a historic and sacred connection with the Hebrew Bible (or Tanakh) and that this Bible begins with Genesis and ends with Chronicles. In contrast, the Old Testament of Christianity ends with Malachi, and the Bible continues to include a New Testament. These are just two differences among many. Or, by comparison, we will find that both faiths have strong connections to charity and social justice. These are comparisons and contrasts that you will learn from any comparative religions class. I find this kind of study fascinating, but this book is not that sort of study. In this book I am much more interested in the borders between Jews and Christians. These are different from the borders between Judaism and Christianity. It is important, first and foremost, to notice that not all Jews represent Judaism in the same way. Among the many examples I could give to illustrate, I will point out two.

Judaism is historically invested in the belief in one God: "Hear, O Israel: The LORD our God, the LORD is one" (Deut. 6:4). This belief is foundational to Judaism and is recited as such in synagogues all over the world, "Sh'ma Yis'ra'eil Adonai Eloheinu Adonai echad." In this case I have told you something true about Judaism. What I have not told you in this statement is what is true about Jews. Many Jews do not attend synagogue. And many Jews who attend synagogue regularly are openly agnostic. Also, it is becoming increasingly popular for Jews to study and practice Buddhism. And whether they are secular, observant but agnostic, or Buddhist, their status as Jews is not in jeopardy. Among my Jewish conversation partners, it is not uncommon to speak of "Jewish Atheists" (Jews who deny the existence of God) or "JewBus" (Jews who practice Buddhism). There is often no perceived contradiction here as there would be in the title "Christian Atheist." So while Deuteronomy 6:4 provides an important window into Judaism, it does not tell us about all Jews.

Another example is that Judaism is deeply invested in care for the earth in general and the well-being of Israel in particular. In these ways, Judaism teaches that one's place and homeland are integral to one's identity. In modern contexts this teaching often translates to the support of the State of Israel. If you walked into a synagogue—be it Orthodox, Conservative, Reform, or Reconstructionist—you should not be surprised to find Jews praying for the State of Israel. Here I have said something true about modern Judaism. Indeed I have told you something about a great many Jews too. (Approximately 80 percent of self-identifying Jews live in Israel or North America.) But there are also many Jews who are highly critical of the State of Israel. While the statehood of Israel is an important element of modern Judaism, it doesn't tell you the whole story about modern Jews.

The point that Jews often do not represent Judaism was suggested to me in dialogue with a senior colleague in my field, a New Testament scholar and self-described "Yankee Jewish feminist," Amy-Jill Levine. In 2010 I was working toward the publication of a book titled *Soundings in the Religion of Jesus*. I coedited this book with Bruce Chilton (an Episcopal priest and Jesus scholar) and Jacob Neusner (a rabbi and scholar). As I took on the role of main editor for this book, I wrote the first chapter and titled it "Introduction: Allowing Historical Study to Serve Interfaith Dialogue." I saw no problem then with the term interfaith. In one of the final chapters of this book, I was kindly corrected:

> Professor Le Donne speaks of "allowing historical study to serve interfaith dialogue." . . . I have a vocabulary concern. For many Jews involved in such dialogue, the issue is not a "faith" matter. To talk of "faith" or "faith communities" already skews the conversation toward Christian terms. Whereas one is a "Christian" because of some assent to Jesus' soteriological role (whether that soteriology is seen as ethical or eschatological), the vast majority of Jews today are Jews because their mothers are Jews. A number of Jews who participate in dialogue do not do so because of a faith or a belief system. Many enter because they want to correct negative Christian stereotypes, or because they want to understand what Christianity is about. They are not faith-identified (they may well be atheists or agnostics). The "faithful" Jews in the Orthodox spectrum do not typically engage in such dialogue, any more than do Evangelical Christians: they see no point in having religious conversations with those who are either wrong, or heretical, or at best in need of conversion. Rather than "interfaith," perhaps the descriptor "Jewish-Christian (or "Christian-Jewish") Dialogue" would more accurately capture the process and the participants.[11]

She is, of course, right. The term interfaith suggests that members of one faith are interacting with members of another faith. This is a very Christian way to think about Jews. But not all Jews are connected to Judaism by way of faith. Moreover, as I have learned in many other settings, it is impossible for Christianity to dialogue with Judaism. No. When we dialogue, we are particular Christians talking to particular Jews. And as Levine points out, many Jews and Christians would prefer not to dialogue at all. It is important to know who is approaching the border to meet their neighbor and why. We might be close to the mark in describing Judaism as a faith,[12] but we err if we think that all Jews represent a faith community.

So this book will not rehash a comparative religions approach. Not only has that book been written a dozen times over, but a description of the ideals and practices of Judaism will not be able to tell whom you might meet along the many and varied Jewish-Christian borders. Certainly Jews are related to Judaism in any number of ways. As such, this book will explain from time to time what "many Jews" believe or think or do. But this is a book about my encounter with particular Jews and particular elements of Jewish identity. It is a book that explains how this encounter has made me, in my view, a more committed Christian. I will let you be the judge of whether I am closer to the heart of Christianity as a result of my encounter at the borders.

> It is important to know who is approaching the border to meet their neighbor and why.

Christians Are Not Christianity

There is another reason why it is important to realize that Jews are not Judaism. In talking with a perceived "other," one cannot help but see oneself in a new light. In conversations with Jews and in my study of Judaism, I realized that Christians are not Christianity either. We do not embody our highest ideals, nor do we express them ideally.

It is true that we are a product of a divine grace, that we are adopted children of God, and that this identity "in Christ" compels us to live in the world as testimonies of grace. This is insider language and expresses our highest aspirations. I do my best to believe it and to live it. I am convinced that we need to remind ourselves of our collective identity in Christ in the hope that we can lean into it.

It is equally true that we fail to embody grace more often than not. Yes, we are children of grace. We are also crusaders who committed innumerable murders in Rhineland in the year 1096. The Jews in Rhineland were forced to convert at pain of death, chose suicide in many cases, but were murdered in many more cases.[13] We are the Crusades.

We are the frontiersmen who committed genocide of Native Americans with a "biblical" sense of manifest destiny. We are colonists.

We are slave traders and slave owners who justified our systematic rape of Africa by pointing to a selection of Bible passages. We then defended this ideology with civil war. We are Confederates.

We are the Christians who humiliated, assaulted, incarcerated, conducted electroconvulsive experimentation on, and murdered gay people during the twentieth century.[14] We are bullies and worse.

These are things that Christians did. As much as we would like to identify with St. Francis, Roger Williams, William Wilberforce, Frederick Douglass, Mother Teresa, and Desmond Tutu, these stories are only part of our collective identity. Our best individual Christians cannot represent the larger narrative of Christianity. Conversely, our worst individual Christians cannot either. Christianity is both more and less than the sum of its parts.

Along similar lines, Christianity reflects a global complexity. I have lived in America, Canada, England, and Zimbabwe. In America, I have lived in wine country, on a desert island, in a sea of cornfields, and in a postindustrial, depressed urban culture. In each of these contexts I have only glimpsed the many idiosyncrasies of Christian culture. I have never experienced life as a South American Catholic or a South Korean charismatic and I never will. As I write this, there are 2.7 billion Christians; by the time this book is published, there will be more than 2.8 billion. I cannot hope to represent all of these cultures, theologies, and political orientations in Jewish-Christian dialogue. Because of my unique placement, I will write often of American evangelicals. I trust that my readers will know that American evangelicals do not represent Christianity at large.

Add to this complexity the fact that American evangelicals are off script in this new millennium. When you meet a born-again Christian (red state or blue state), he may be an LGBTQ+ activist or she may be a member of the NRA. You can no longer assume social or political sensibility based on the label evangelical. Even if we limit our focus to American Christianity, we are massively diverse. So even though I have lived a little and studied a lot, my experience of Christianity is limited, and this book will reflect my limitations.

> American evangelicals are off script in this new millennium. When you meet a born-again Christian (red state or blue state), he may be an LGBTQ+ activist or she may be a member of the NRA.

Multiplicity of Borders

We must, therefore, talk about Jewish-Christian borders in the plural. The history between Christians and Jews in Brazil will be different from that of Canada (just to name two examples). We should expect, then, that the complexity of Jewish-Christian relations will differ depending on context. In many ways I have more in common with my West Coast, baseball-loving, social-justice-oriented, Jewish friends than I do with my "country-minded" Christian siblings in Queensland, Australia. My shared culture with many American Jews surely colors my perspective in any number of ways. That said, I continue to be surprised by how different I am from my Jewish friends. Geographical location is an important border, but it is only one type of border.

Historic and important borders between Christians and Jews include language, intermarriage, conversion, violence, diet, Christology, eschatology, and sacred texts. We must also factor in orientations to time, location, embodiment, ritual, and memory—just to name a few. This book will touch the surface of a few of these topics and bypass others altogether. I do not think that any single book could be comprehensive, and surely this book is not.

I have chosen only a few borders to explore: pilgrim and stranger, always winter and always Christmas, Jesus and genocide, dogma and underdogma, anti-Judaism and philo-Judaism, laughter and intimacy, tolerance and love, and belief and belonging. In each chapter I assume that there is indeed a connection between the two ideas. Some of these connections, like tolerance and love, might seem readily apparent. Others, like Jesus and genocide, might seem worlds apart. This book will explain how these ideas relate and what they have to do with Christians on the borders and with the borders of Christianity. I will share what I have learned about these topics in Jewish-Christian conversation and how these conversations have enhanced my faith.

Saved?

Before moving forward, I should also say a brief word about the subtitle of this book: *How Journeys along Jewish-Christian Borders Saved My Faith in God*. I realize that I am playing with the Christian concept of soteriology. It might be assumed that I think that I have been saved *from* something: hell, unbelief, apostasy, reality television, or something almost as horrible. This is not what I mean by being saved.

The act of saving can have a sense of preservation. When I value something—let's say an old coin—I might preserve it in a jar or a drawer or a binder. But faith is not something that can be stowed away and "saved" in this way. If you want to save faith, it must be nurtured, challenged, and enhanced. In this way, saving faith is more like child rearing than coin collecting. In this metaphor, the child is me as a child of God (to borrow a biblical concept). Faith saving, in my view, is closer to helping something valuable evolve into something more than it was. This book reflects on a few ways that my conversations with Jewish friends and my study of Judaism have made me something more than a mere Christian.

On the Border of Pilgrim and Stranger

> [H]e looked up and saw that he was so far away from home that he was in a part of the road he had never seen before. Then came the sound of a musical instrument, from behind it seemed, very sweet and very short, as if it were one plucking of a string or one note of a bell, and after it a full clear voice—and it sounded so high and strange that he thought it was very far away, further than a star. The voice said, Come.
>
> —C. S. LEWIS, *THE PILGRIM'S REGRESS*

> The fool who traveled is better off than the wise man who stayed home.
>
> —RASHI

Sidewalk to Synagogue

One of the realities of pilgrimage is border crossing. Whether it is a physical or spiritual journey, borderlands must be navigated. Boundary markers must be interpreted. Some borders suggest new life, progress, or possibility. My memory of the concrete tunnel that opened up to Candlestick Park was like that. Upon entry, that concrete tunnel was only nostalgic in that it promised something better, greener beyond. Or you might know what I mean if you've ever ascended the hills of Bodega until the visual barrier is broken, revealing the Pacific Ocean. Those rolling hills boast their own beauty. But they also border something greater.

Other borders suggest insecurity, anxiety, or painful departure. Life after a lover's death is such a border crossing. Or imagine the return home of a daughter who has been estranged for too long from her parents. Some borders have metal detectors and checkpoints and offer no guarantees of easy passage. Some are literal barriers, all but impassable.

Borders can take many forms; they can be physical, temporal, cultural, or a combination of many forms. Most of the borders I discuss in this book are religious in nature or at least have a religious dimension. Most are conceptual, rather than physical. But I will begin with a seemingly mundane border: a sidewalk.

I sat in the passenger seat of Larry's Prius *en route* to Temple Emanuel. Larry Behrendt is a friend of mine, Jewish, actively invested in the well-being of his Christian friends, and an all-around good guy. I had been to many synagogues, but never his. There was nothing particularly sacred or strange about the journey. Judging by the tenor of our conversation, we could have been going to a little league game. It didn't feel like much of a pilgrimage. We were in Beverly Hills, after all—not exactly a cross-cultural experience for a kid raised in wine country. Yet as we crossed the border from sidewalk to synagogue, an unmistakable boundary marker waited for us.

In front of a lovely little chapel was an armed guard. Standing erect, blue uniform, head shorn, expressionless. I don't know enough about firearms to know the model of his gun. I do remember being impressed—and a little disturbed—by the display. I decided to say nothing for the moment.

My first experience at this Reform synagogue was a Buddhist-styled session of meditation. The rabbi guided us in a practice called "mindfulness," wherein we were encouraged to be present and observant within ourselves. I attempted to focus on something other than the man with a gun just beyond that threshold. I am not inordinately squeamish about guns; it just seemed odd in a place of worship. Did this armed guard provide comfort or distraction for my fellow meditators?

After the meditation we left the chapel across the same sidewalk and walked by the same guard. The Sabbath service would be in another building across the street.

I turned to Larry, "What's up with him?"

Larry doesn't often play coy, but he did today. "Who?"

"The armed guard."

"He's here to protect us from our enemies."

Larry's eyes twinkled just enough to let me know that he had more to say on this topic. We turned the corner and walked into the foyer; there was another armed guard with a similar uniform and posture. Worship was about to begin, so our dialogue about borders would have to wait.

As we entered the synagogue, I reflected on the history of Christians and Jews. For centuries, reaching back to the violence of medieval Christianity, Jews have lived with Christian neighbors who were not invested in their well-being. Indeed, too many of these Christians deliberately intimidated their neighbors and worse. Jews and Christians generally get along these days, but this positive development is relatively recent. Even so, the intimidating shadow of Christianity still looms large.

> For centuries, reaching back to the violence of medieval Christianity, Jews have lived with Christian neighbors who were not invested in their well-being.

Consider the population disparity. There are now over 2.7 billion Christians. Contrast this with 14 million Jews worldwide. We measure Jews in millions and Christians in billions.[1] Even if only one out of every hundred Christians were anti-Semitic (1 percent of

2.7 billion), this would make for 27 million anti-Semitic Christians in the world. Even if my low estimate is close to the mark—and this doesn't even include non-Christian anti-Semites—there are far more anti-Semites in the world than there are Jews.

So Larry says "to protect us from our enemies."

In my experience, Jews tend to respond differently to religious borders than do Christians. Jews have a long history of living near neighbors who curse them. This is bad enough. But when your neighbors outnumber you on all sides, such curses can become perilous. History—even recent history—suggests that many of these neighbors wish the Jews' extinction. So sometimes armed guards are employed.

Extinction is not a necessary concern for Christianity. We may have unhealthy denominations, but there is no danger of Christianity's imminent demise. In contrast, Jewish extinction is a real-world concern for many Jews. There are many different elements that feed this concern, including Israel's political instability and intermarriage with non-Jews. The cultural memory of the Holocaust looms large, and its impact is still unfolding. Too much was lost—too many families, too many people—for Jews not to think hard about the possibility of Jewish extinction. Related to this concern, although this might be difficult for many Christians to hear, is the problem of Christian evangelism. For many Jews, the Christian drive to seek converts is a threat. It may not be the only factor, but it is related to the worry nonetheless.

Therefore, many Jews relate to borders differently than do Christians. More to the point, there is little comfort in the knowledge that these borders are populated by Christians.

I take no pleasure in saying this, but a great many people have been trampled over in the name of Christian pilgrimage. Countless Jews have encountered Christians who are on some crusade, quest, or adventure. Even when we have good intentions—and this cannot be assumed—we Christians leave a heavy footprint when we travel. The medieval rabbi Rashi speaks the truth when he says, "The fool who traveled is better off than the wise man who stayed home." But I wonder whether the people who encounter the fool are better off.

Peter Bellini is my colleague at United Theological Seminary; he teaches missiology to aspiring Christian leaders. Peter puts it like this: "For the last five hundred or so years, evangelization has often coat-tailed on colonial exploration and exploitation. We spent the better part of those years making a mess; I think it might be better to move a bit more slowly." I would echo this assessment and add that Christianity's traditional hostility toward our Jewish neighbors is older still.

> Even when we have good intentions—and this cannot be assumed—we Christians leave a heavy footprint when we travel.

The Greek word *parepidemos* can mean both "pilgrim" and "stranger." The Latin word *peregrinus* can mean both "pilgrim" and "stranger." Historically speaking, we Christians have been both at the same time. We have warranted suspicion.

After worship and before a nice meal, Larry and I talked about my experience at his synagogue. Without a doubt, I had experienced something sacred. To the extent that I experience God, which is a struggle for me, I had that experience that day. I was surprised by this. I was surprised not because it had been in a synagogue but because my experience of God is most often silence. This experience had been a gift. But I said none of this to Larry. Perhaps later, over drinks that night.

We passed the armed guards again along the sidewalk. Larry and I repositioned ourselves in his Prius. The streets of southern

California served as my reentry into the "Christian" world. I saw no evidence of enemies lurking, unless you include the odd Dodgers-capped pedestrian. Our conversation continued.

"Is the guard necessary?"

"I would love it if you'd ask my rabbi that question!"

"Why? What will she say?"

"I would like to hear what she says, actually. I think that she's convinced that the guard is necessary. I think it sends the wrong message."

"Is this a common practice at synagogues? I've never seen it before."

I was shocked to learn that it is not uncommon for synagogues in urban settings to employ armed guards. Larry asked, "Don't megachurches do the same?" I didn't rightly know the answer to his question.[2] Most of my church experience had been in smaller congregations. Some larger churches had employed a security guard, but I'd never seen them armed. I told him that I have never been in church with an armed guard—not once in forty years.

> Exile is not something to be celebrated. The song of the open road becomes a lament when it is forced upon you.

Like their Christian counterparts, Jews have a long history of pilgrimage. But not by choice. In the Jewish story, Jews become strangers by forced displacement. It has been said often that Jews are people who commemorate the exodus. From Canaan, to Babylon, to Brazil, to twentieth-century Europe, Jews pass on the memory of their sojourn in the wilderness. Exile is not something to be celebrated. The song of the open road becomes a lament when it is forced upon you. Indeed, the Jewish story of border crossing contains few happy endings. As I write this, many Jews in France are now feeling it is dangerous to remain.

Many Jews live in a world of borders that most Christians can hardly imagine. We Christians are prone to trespass onto sacred ground unwittingly in our wanderlust.

Only days after our conversation about the armed guard, Facebook alerted me to terrible news. A shooter shouting "Heil Hitler" stormed into a Jewish community center in Kansas.[3] The man shot and killed three people. I immediately emailed the news link to Larry. He wrote back, "It is wildly inappropriate for me to think this, but . . . this ties into so many different things we've talked about." I wrote back, "I was thinking the same thing."

These two memories are now linked: the armed guard in Beverly Hills and the victims in Kansas. I don't feel any wiser for the association, but I do recognize that the border between synagogue and sidewalk is more complicated than I had previously imagined.

Concerning Pilgrims

Jesus banded together "followers." Mark's gospel suggests a group on the move. The apostles were those "sent" by Jesus.[4] They began from Israel and journeyed to the far reaches of the Roman Empire. This, the story of the New Testament, suggests that a pebble dropped in Galilee created waves felt all over the Mediterranean. The story of pilgrimage was a favorite of the early church. *The Shepherd of Hermas*—a popular second-century fiction—used pilgrimage as a metaphor for the Christian life.

A Christian letter from the same period suggests that Christians are never truly at home in their native lands: "[Christians] live each in their native land but as though they were not really at home there. They share in all duties as citizens and suffer all hardships as strangers. Every foreign country is a fatherland to them, and every fatherland a foreign land . . . They dwell on earth but they are citizens of heaven" (*Letter to Diognetus*, 5).

While some Christians were making literal pilgrimages to Jerusalem as early as the fourth century, Gregory of Nyssa (c. 335–c. 95) taught that the most important pilgrimage is the interior one to God. Perhaps the most influential of the Christian theologians, Augustine of Hippo (354–430), suggested that the literal Jerusalem acts as a sign for the heavenly Jerusalem. "Witness the prayer of the whole city of God in its pilgrim state," writes St. Augustine. "For it cries to God by the mouth of all its members, 'Forgive us our debts as we forgive our debtor'" (*City of God* XIX.27). Here Augustine preaches that the Christian community exists in a "pilgrim state." Accordingly, there is no literal "Christian city" but rather a Christian way in the world.

Pilgrimage was a favorite theme for medieval Christian authors.[5] John Bunyan (1628–88) gave it new life with his work *The Pilgrim's Progress*. The theme emerged again in the 1800s with the multi-authored Russian work *The Way of a Pilgrim*. These stories remind us that we are a people without any single holy place. We sing that we're "just passing through." Our true home is heaven. "Further up and further in!" proclaims C. S. Lewis through the voice of Aslan.

Quentin Tarantino's *Pulp Fiction* portrays the conversion of a gangster named Jules Winnfield. After Jules feels "the touch of God," he explains to his partner in crime what he's going to do with his newly transformed life: he is just going to walk the earth like Cain from *Kung Fu* . . . walk until God puts him where God wants him to be.

Christians are pilgrims. It's in our spiritual DNA. Sometimes we're gun-toting crusaders like Jules Winnfield. At other times we're more like the passive wanderer in Lewis's *The Pilgrim's*

Regress. More often than not, we are a combination of both. We struggle with our identities on the road like Bilbo Baggins, that Tookish burglar imagined by Lewis's famous Catholic friend. Whatever our posture, we tend to idealize our resolutions to walk from place to place, meet people, get into adventures.

Christian pilgrims tend to have an impact on the people they meet and the places they occupy. Not only is this impact not always welcomed; it is all too often to the detriment of our neighbors.

On the Way

Long before anyone had heard the word Christian, a band of Jewish disciples called the Way followed a rabbi named Jesus. They continued to claim Jesus as their anointed leader even after his death. Perhaps they were actually following Peter or James or John, but they believed that their way was mapped by Jesus.

Given my brief sketch of Christian pilgrimage, you might think that the Way was an apt Christian name for the followers of Jesus. But in truth this name emerges from Jewish sensibilities.

Jesus' followers were not the only Jews to call themselves the Way. The sect of Jews who collected and authored the Dead Sea Scrolls also called themselves the Way. This group created a community in the Judean desert, near the Dead Sea, at a place called Khirbet Qumran. They believed themselves to preserve the true priesthood for service within the Jerusalem temple. They hoped for and expected the Creator to provide a new and purified temple in Jerusalem. When that day came, they thought, the true priesthood would return to their God-given vocations. This, they believed, would fit hand in glove with the national turn toward repentance and purity. In short, they were hoping for a way back to the Holy City. It was their group that would bring holiness back to the City. At least in a spiritual and metaphorical sense, they were hoping for a way home.

We see a similar hope in the preaching of another Jewish prophet during this period: John the Baptist. "Prepare the way for the Lord, make straight paths for him" (Matt. 3:3). Borrowing from the prophet Isaiah, John was preaching about repentance and providing a way toward purity in worship. When John preached about the way of the Lord, he hoped for the day—the sooner the better—when the Lord of Israel would return and lead the people of Israel to a restored and pure state.

Many Jews in the first century were awaiting a return. (The Hebrew word *shuv* can mean both "return" and "repent.") It was time for a return: a return to political autonomy, a return from foreign influence, a return to the ways of Moses' instructions for life in the Land. When first-century Jews talked about the way, they often meant "the way of life in the Land."

I cannot help but wonder if this hope for the Way also gave birth to the apostles of the book of Acts. In Acts 1:6 the apostles ask Jesus, "Lord, are you at this the time going to restore the kingdom to Israel?" They, as many Jews would have, hoped for restored autonomy and for a way to experience God in a pure state of worship.

So when did this mentality change for Christians? When did Christians stop hoping for a way of life in the Land and seek, instead, a way to the afterlife? When did Christianity become an outward-focused mission with little regard for a single holy place? This—what scholars call "the parting of the ways"—is much debated. It was once thought that the early Christians forsook their Jewish siblings in a dramatic divorce during the life of Paul. Many scholars now think that Jewish followers of Jesus preserved their cultural, ethnic, and religious heritage long after Paul's life and career.

The historical problem of "the parting of the ways" is complicated and will not be solved anytime soon. I certainly won't solve it here, but I think that it must have had something to do with the Christian notion that they could experience God in the spiritual temple of their community. The early chapters of Acts tell us that the Jewish followers of Jesus—the Way—continued to worship in the temple. (Later in the narrative, Paul too returns to the temple.) This should not surprise us, as they were Jews living in and near Jerusalem. But, in contrast to many Jews of the time, the followers of Jesus believed that they had become a *spiritual* temple. When Christians gathered and worshiped, they called themselves the temple of the Holy Spirit. This allowed them to see Jerusalem as a home base, but their new identity was every bit as portable as the tabernacle of the early Israelites. Instead of looking for a way into the Land, they found their new identity along the way.

> So when did this mentality change for Christians? When did Christians stop hoping for a way of life in the Land and seek, instead, a way to the afterlife?

This cannot and should not be heard as an explanation for the many and varied differences between Christians and Jews. My sketch here is too simplistic to be anything more than a partial explanation. It might explain, in a limited way, why many Christians cross borders with relative ease without much regard for life in the Land.

When You're a Stranger

One of my Jewish mentors is a sociologist and historian. He tells me that the best educations are acquired in proximity to a border.

When one lives on a border—especially one that is marked by cultural differences—there is a greater possibility of seeing how your neighbor lives and thinks. Of course, it takes more than a border to provide an education. It is possible to live near a border and learn nothing of significance about one's neighbor. This observation is one of possibility: living in a borderland affords you the possibility of education. Becoming truly cosmopolitan involves adopting a curious and receptive posture. It also requires a suspension (at least partially) of fear.

In my brief description of Christian origins, I suggested that many Christians cross borders with ease. In some ways this is still true of modern Christians. But it is often because we are unaware of the fault lines we have imposed on the Western landscape. How can we tell who has been wounded by Catholic pedophilia scandals? How many among our neighbors associate American Christians with rampant gun culture and repeated tragedy? How many have been alienated by our traditionally fearful and hostile stances against the LGBTQ+ community? These questions defy easy answers. Too often we do not know where we have trespassed and where the fault lines are as a result. Could it be that when we're debating public prayer, just to name one example, our neighbors distrust us for other legitimate reasons? Sometimes we think that we're discussing one kind of border (e.g., prayer), but a dozen other fault lines conspire against a simple conversation.

Here is another example. When many conservative Christians enter into discussion with Reform Jews, an obvious religious border is occupied. I have found that the Christians are most interested in matters related to Christology. We often wonder, What do Jews think about Jesus? What many Christians do not know is that there are dozens of other fault lines that Christianity has created that hinder any simple discussion of Jesus. Perhaps more pressing for many Reform Jews is this question: why is the LGBTQ+ issue so important to Christians? This is not a universal fault line. It is, however, true that most Reform Jews see great virtue and necessity in LGBTQ+ advocacy.[6] Complicating this matter, most evangelicals are highly invested in traditional gender borders (even though it is not a central doctrinal issue in our creeds). Most Christians, however, are unaware that this particular fault line has affected multiple religious borders around us.

In this example there are at least three very important borders. There is the historic border created by our various orientations to Jesus. This seems an obvious religious border. There is also the complicated border between evangelicals and LGBTQ+ advocacy. Most Christians readily admit that these topics have created cultural borders between our neighbors and us. The third border remains all but invisible to many evangelicals: it might never occur to us that Reform Jews care much less about Jesus and much more about the problems of homophobia.

Or consider another illustration of fear and lack of awareness. American Christians as a whole are becoming ever more Islamophobic. This probably coincides with a general resurgence of xenophobia in America. While the borders between Christians and Muslims have become (quite literally) militarized, Christians continue to lack awareness of who's who in the Muslim world. Do we know the differences between Sunnis and Shiites? Are we aware of America's role in the creation of certain extremist factions? Do we know or even care that Sikhism is not an Abrahamic religion? Even when Christians are

> Even when Christians are vigilantly concerned with borders, it does not necessarily increase our intelligence of our neighbors. It is often the case, however, that increased curiosity and eager education can supplant fear.

vigilantly concerned with borders, it does not necessarily increase our intelligence of our neighbors. It is often the case, however, that increased curiosity and eager education can supplant fear.

C. S. Lewis illustrated this as he wrote about one of his personal fears. "I would rather meet a ghost than a tarantula." Insects in general gave Lewis nightmares as a child. As such, one of the borders he most feared was an open window; the world of spiders and insects was right outside. This all changed in his teens, when he became fascinated with entomology, and he went on to say "while my entomological period lasted my fear almost vanished, and I am inclined to think a real objective curiosity will usually have this cleansing effect."[7]

Some people find a dangerous border just beyond the threshold of their home. For some the complicated borders between gender and sexuality are frightening. For others it is the border between urban and rural life. My own borders—the ones that cause me fear—relate to those around the ivory tower. For me a safe world would be one where I could research and write what I please without the fear of the condemnation from the church. The borders between the seminary and sanctuary cause me no little anxiety. Sometimes I feel that I reveal the least of myself around fellow Christians for fear of the sideways glance when I tell them what sort of books I write. I have taken to examining the church scientifically as Lewis did with spiders to manage my fear.

But stepping out of our homes is often times a necessity. I think that it is equally necessary to learn at least enough about Islam to embrace the varieties of Muslims we will meet and those whom we will never meet. Our fear of the borders between urban and rural life may well cause a great deal of political vitriol. Learning about this border may heal us in many ways. For my part, I know that I need greater intimacy within the church however much risk is involved in the relationship. Moreover, as I have suggested, Christians will often step across borders despite our anxiety, because this is just what Christians do. It is part of our spiritual identity to journey and sojourn and journey again. So we must ask ourselves, Do we step out in fear or curiosity? Because the answer to this question may well determine the sort of relationships we will create along the way.

Another matter that relates to borders is self-awareness. Consider differences in regional accents. There is perhaps nothing that betrays a stranger more than a foreign accent. It will not tell you how long the stranger has been in the area. (Perhaps she has been a "local" for decades.) It will, however, create a noticeable difference as soon as she opens her mouth. I have spent much of my adult life outside of the United States. During these years I was always aware of my accent and constantly being associated with American stereotypes. Being a foreigner is like bringing a border with you wherever you go. Of course, accents rarely reveal enough about the stranger.

I am a Californian who completed my graduate education in Canada and my PhD in England. I had friends in Canada who would attempt an American accent by mimicking George W. Bush. This was playfully meant to mock my speech patterns. I found it amusing for a different reason: to my ear, my northern Californian accent sounded very different from a Texas accent. In my PhD days, my Church of England rector heard my accent and thought I was from Ireland. Apparently some Englishmen have trouble distinguishing American and Irish accents at times. For our part, many Americans have trouble distinguishing English and Australian accents.

These are all quirks of crossing unfamiliar borders, and we learn as we go. We can hardly fault strangers for not being fluent in the nuances of dialect. The misstep that is most troubling and that most hinders borderland education is a lack of self-awareness. I have heard far too often from certain Californians that "we don't have an accent." It will sound absurd to almost everyone reading this, but there is a popular mythology where I'm from that Californians simply lack any regional accent. Notice the ridiculous lack of self-awareness in this claim! In truth there are probably a dozen different accents in California. But with a lack of self-awareness, many people cannot hear their own inflections. What is absolutely necessary in our education along borders is first to become self-aware. Even more important, we must realize that self-awareness is always ongoing and unfolding.

Pilgrimage and Power

Christians have enormous power. We have power over the way our history is told. We have power over the Christianized calendar. We have power to influence governance and to advocate for those without social privilege. We have the capacity to experience the power of God through ecstatic worship and social justice. Because of my own interests and because it relates more closely to religious borders, I will focus on social justice.

> What is absolutely necessary in our education along borders is first to become self-aware.

Alienation is a condition that knows no border. The Christian belief that we are strangers in a strange land can—I will not say does—coax us toward a posture of social justice. If we are ourselves aliens rather than heroes, we can better identify with the alienated. Peruvian Catholic theologian Gustavo Gutiérrez reminds us that Christianity, if understood as a message that casts off institutional power (rather than accumulating and defending it), can indeed be good news for strangers.[8] In his view, Christians must forsake places of power and false security, and themselves identify with the oppressed. This, of course, requires a border crossing for many affluent Christians.

Theologian James Hal Cone has applied this insight within American race-relations. Cone argued that white Christians must "become" black in order to be Christians. This seemed an impossible border to cross for many of Cone's readers. Christians may cross borders with ease, but some borders are easier than others. When he was writing in the late 1960s, Cone's program was met with resistance, even by those who were sympathetic to civil rights. Many liberal, white Christians were quite happy to offer help to their black siblings, but it seemed as though Cone was making "blackness" a necessary requirement. Cone explained: "Being black in America has very little to do with skin color. To be black means that your heart, your soul, your mind, and your body are where the dispossessed are. . . . Therefore, being reconciled to God does not mean that one's skin is physically black. It essentially depends on the color of your heart, soul, and mind."[9]

Both Gutiérrez and Cone invite Christians to cross borders to find a deeper and richer virtue within the Good News. Again, the purpose of the border crossing is not to act heroically; it is a necessary path born of pain.

Or consider this example from the life of theologian Frances Young. During years of struggling with God over her son's physical disability, she writes, "through my son I have been brought to a very different place." Young continues, "I stand alongside him as a vulnerable creature, disabled and mortal, knowing my creaturely limitations and my lack of knowledge, especially of God."[10] Here Young takes a step further than Gutiérrez. Not only is she powerless to occupy the role of savior—she cannot "save" her son from his pain—she becomes herself disabled by her "lack of knowledge, especially of God." Her pilgrimage has been mapped by pain and follows a path into uncertainty.

Upon reading Young I found her pilgrimage to be especially comforting. Her pilgrimage as a Christian has been mapped by a lack of knowledge of God. In reading her words I gained a greater awareness that my life within God's silence is not something less spiritual or less holy. I would not describe my way in terms of suffering. But the self-emptying ways described by Gutiérrez, Cone, and Young are mapped by pain and point a way forward for me.

In these ways, the borders of Christian identity are renegotiated, redefined, indeed crossed over as motivated by suffering. They do not represent the zeal of heroism or sentimentalized calls to adventure. They do perhaps strike closer to the heart of Christian beginnings. While we were still strangers, while we were still enemies, St. Paul tells us, God through a "son of God," suffered. This will seem banal to Christian ears, but it must be heard in a different way. Acquiring cultural, political, and religious power has not worked well for Christianity.

Hebrew Bible scholar and multifaith chaplain Joel Lohr is a Christian who has spent most of his life along Jewish-Christian borders. I am blessed to call him a friend and have learned a great deal from him. Joel recently preached on Philippians 2:3, where Paul writes, "Do nothing out of selfish ambition or vain conceit. Rather, in humility value others above yourselves." Joel asked, "What if Christians learned to apply this wisdom to our religious neighbors? What if we began to value our religious neighbors above ourselves?" I do not rightly know the answer to this. My guess is that many Christians will find such a self-emptying path troubling. But, in light of the path that Paul prescribes in

Philippians 2:3–8, it might be the only path worthy to be called Christian.

Could it be that we Christians must cede power—especially religious power—to our less powerful neighbors? I am tempted to answer yes.

My friend Rabbi Brad Hirschfield has a different view, and I find it challenging. Brad observes that some Christians focus on the Jesus of resurrected power. When they experience Jesus in their lives, they experience the one who conquers death. Other Christians focus on Jesus as the disempowered, emptied, and crucified one. (Cone, Gutiérrez, and Young might be explained this way.) Or perhaps we see Jesus as the rabbi ministering to the powerless people of Israel. Rabbi Hirschfield wonders whether there may be a connection between these different views of Jesus and two very different Christian approaches to power.

My guess is that many Christians will find such a self-emptying path troubling. But, in light of the path that Paul prescribes in Philippians 2:3–8, it might be the only path worthy to be called Christian.

He asks, Do those who focus on Jesus' power tend to see other powerful people as models? Conversely, do those who focus on Jesus' disempowerment tend to see Christ in the least powerful people? If there is a connection between our images of Jesus and our approaches to power, there are also two subtle dangers lurking. Do conservatives tend to see goodness in the powerful simply because they have power? Do liberals tend to see goodness in the weak simply because they are weak? Here is a short excerpt of our conversation:

BRAD: The worship of power is clearly idolatrous and dangerous. The worship of powerlessness is just as idolatrous and dangerous.

ANTHONY: But Brad, the rise of Christianity has tended to be very bad for the Jews. Our acquisition of power has almost always had a negative impact on Jews and Judaism. Don't you want more Christians who eschew power wherever they can?

BRAD: I believe the world needs people who neither idolize power nor powerlessness. I believe we need people, including Christians, who embrace power, but who do so realizing that its use must be measured not only against their own ideas and ideals, but at least to some extent against the ideas and ideals of those with whom they do not agree.[11]

Of course Brad is right that we should make more of an effort to be in conversation with our neighbors. I am not certain, however, that Christians should be trusted to be self-aware or aware of the ideas and ideals of others. That said, Brad reminds me that hope is indeed a Christian ideal. For his part, he has hope for Christians and Christianity in spite of our history.

Perhaps we should hear Rabbi Hirschfield's confidence as an invitation to be better stewards of our social placement. How will we know how to value others above ourselves if we do not first (a) know ourselves and (b) know our neighbors? In our history of pilgrimages and sojourns, Christians have gained many more neighbors than we would have otherwise. We therefore have greater opportunity and responsibility to learn from our borders.

In writing this chapter I tried to practice what I am now preaching. As such I asked four Jewish scholars (all my senior and all who are invested in the increased friendship of Jews and Christians) to read over a draft of this chapter. These readers do not (and cannot) represent Judaism at large, much less the many and varied voices of Jews at large. They are, however, important voices along my own personal borders. I will not name them here. Rather I will mention something that three of the four readers mentioned.

Along the lines of Rabbi Hirschfield above, three of my readers had misgivings with the notion that Christians should eschew power simply on principle. The common refrain was that it may benefit Christian spirituality to cast off power, but such a practice has the danger of doing more harm than good. Becoming overly passive is not an admirable goal. Moreover, too much power in any person's hands can be a corrupting influence. So why would we want to corrupt our neighbors with the power that has corrupted us? I will add one more point that I've learned not from my Jewish mentors but from my students who are social activists and African American preachers: not every Christian should be asked to cede power.

I take this critique seriously and will continue to consider its merits. I have also learned from my Jewish mentors that Jews and Christians need not agree on everything. Interreligious conversations are most fruitful when both sides maintain their distinct identities. I am also aware of my own place of social privilege and I do not presume that every person reading these words enjoys the same privilege.

So I offer the following insight as food for thought. It is not something that I necessarily prescribe or lay down in a determinative way.

Wherever pilgrimage is concerned and wherever religious territory is disputed, the Christian default position should be to eschew power. I have in mind almost all forms of pilgrimage including the settling of foreign lands, evangelization, spiritual self-realization, and so on. This process of self-emptying may well introduce its own unique problems. I am convinced, however, that the problems of advancing religious territory by force have not worked well for Christian witness. Indeed, if done by force, it probably ceases to be a pilgrimage and becomes a crusade. Both in our physical global presence and our spiritual journeys, we are most Christian when we hold our self-interest most lightly.

Henri Nouwen reminds us that even those in positions of leadership (i.e., those most clearly having and beholden to religious power) must seek the "downward-moving way of Jesus." Nouwen writes:

> Here we touch the most important quality of Christian leadership in the future. It is not a leadership of power and control, but a leadership of powerlessness and humility. . . . I, obviously, am not speaking about psychologically weak leadership in which Christian leaders are simply the passive victims of the manipulations of their milieu. No, I am speaking of a leadership in which power is constantly abandoned in favor of love. It is a true spiritual leadership. Powerlessness and humility in the spiritual life do not refer to people who have no spine and who let everyone else make decisions for them. They refer to people who are so deeply in love with Jesus that they are ready to follow him wherever he guides them, always trusting that, with him, they will find life and find it abundantly.[12]

Notice that Nouwen's "downward-moving way" is a way that follows Jesus. As such, he preserves the language of spiritual pilgrimage. Notice also that Nouwen contrasts power and love. (This points us to one of the final chapters of this book that concerns the border of love and tolerance.) Finally, Nouwen's vision for the Christian pilgrim is neither overly passive nor easily manipulated. To my mind what Nouwen describes is the difference between sojourning together with neighbors and crusading toward exploitable territory. The way of Jesus must be closer to the former.

On the Border of Always Winter and Always Christmas

> Christmas cards in general and the whole vast commercial drive called "Xmas" are one of my pet abominations. . . . If it were my business to have a "view" on this, I should say that I much approve of merrymaking. But what I approve of much more is everybody minding his own business.
>
> —C. S. LEWIS, *LETTER TO MILWARD*, 1955

> I grew up in a gentler, slower time. . . . Christmases were years apart, and now it's about five months from one to the next.
>
> —GARRISON KEILLOR

Right Facts, Wrong Narrative

One of the first things that Christians learn about Jews in dialogue is the diversity of Jewishness. Rabbi Hirschfield reminds me: "You've probably heard the old joke of 'two Jews, three opinions'? Well it's not just a joke. The value of divergence of views among Jews derives from generations and generations valuing Talmudic dialogue. In Talmudic study one learns to value the conversation more than the conclusion."[1]

Amy-Jill Levine reminds me: "Judaism has no pope." Even if most modern Jews come to widespread agreement on a particular topic, there is never a final, authoritative word spoken *ex cathedra*.[2] In my own experience, learning about Jewish diversity (both past and present) has taught me something about the importance of Christian diversity. In my conversations with Jewish friends I often find myself saying, "Well, I can only speak for myself on this," or, "Now, you might get a different answer from a Brazilian Catholic or Russian Orthodox Christian, but . . ."

One thing that creates differences among Christians is the diversity of how we remember or fail to remember the Christian calendar. For example, my wife and I have learned that choosing to celebrate St. Nicholas Day (December 6) with our children has consequences.

We were on our way back from California after Thanksgiving. My daughter was seven and my son was four. I love this story because it reflects my son's no-nonsense personality and my daughter's eager and honest mind. It also illustrates a simple cultural misunderstanding. In this story my little family was in an airport in central Illinois.

When we visit family, we tend to avoid Christmas travel. My parents both grew up on dairy farms, so they have never celebrated Christmas morning with much dedication. Dairy farmers milk the cows in the morning. Our tradition has always involved a Christmas Eve party instead. My wife and I have created our own Christmas morning traditions in the Midwest and try to visit the grandparents on Thanksgiving. This migration pattern inevitably places my family in midwestern airports just as the Christmas season ramps up to a fever pitch.

At Gate 1 in the Springfield airport a kindly, grandmotherly Illinoisan struck up a conversation with my son. She learned that my son had just returned from California. She learned what sort of foods he likes best at Thanksgiving. Then she asked him what she thought was an innocent question: "Have you written your letter to Santa Claus yet?"

My son can deadpan (it is an emerging spiritual gift) and did so without hesitation. "No. Santa's dead." The poor woman thinly veiled her horror with a look of sympathy. "Oh dear, no he's not!" "Yes he is." "Who told you that, sweetie?" "My sister." "I'm sure she didn't mean it." At this point my daughter interjected to set the record straight. "Yes, I did." To this, the woman had no reply and looked incredulously at my wife, not sure whether she should feel sorry for the parent or the children. My wife, Sarah—who hates misunderstandings of all kinds—tried to explain, but the damage was done.

Sarah's side of the story is that she was teaching our kids about the historical figure St. Nicholas (c. 270–343). As my daughter will tell you, St. Nicholas—upon whom the mythology of Santa Claus is based—died a very long time ago. This bit of history had obviously made an impression on my children. To the dismay of our Springfield sojourner, my children held forth as evangelists of Yuletide death.

Truth needs to be contextualized to avoid misunderstanding. On the one hand, my wife and I should have done a better job communicating the difference between Santa Claus and St. Nicholas. On the other, the woman might have done better to avoid an argument with my four-year-old son. Assumptions on both sides shaped our misunderstandings of Santa's demise. Nobody at Gate 1 was waging a war on Christmas, but facts framed in the wrong way can lead to such notions.

My feeling is that the truth is tricky and sometimes facts deceive. This is seen most clearly in misunderstandings between neighboring cultures.

Advent

Not all hymns are worth the time it takes to sing them. I feel about many hymns as Lewis once did: "fifth-rate poems set to sixth-rate music."[3] My favorite Christmas song, however, happens to be a hymn.

"O Come, O Come Emmanuel" is a very old, Christian plea for the incarnation as the nights of winter grow longer. The tune is at least as old as the fifteenth century. When Latin lyrics were attached to it, the plea was *Veni, Veni, Emmanuel*. The hymn is hauntingly medieval, sounding almost like a funeral dirge. Consider some of the vocabulary used: ransom; mourns in lonely exile; Satan's tyranny; depths of hell; the grave; the gloomy clouds of night; death's dark shadows; the path to misery. It is also full of hope. Famously, the chorus sings:

> Rejoice! Rejoice! Emmanuel,
> Shall come to thee, O Israel.

It has been almost twenty years since my two semesters of Latin, but I can still read bits and pieces of the 1710 lyrics:[4]

> *Gaude, gaude, Emmanuel,*
> *nascetur pro te, Israel!*

Gaude is an imperative verb: "Rejoice!" This much is translated faithfully in most English hymnals. *Nascetur* (as I reacquaint myself with my Latin dictionary) is not "shall come," as most hymnals render it. *Nascetur pro te* is better translated "shall be born for you." This of course reminds us that Jesus did not simply arrive; the nativity stories of Matthew and Luke boast that Jesus was born.

Simply put, Israel is told to be glad in this chorus. The birth of Jesus is cause for the rejoicing of Israel. In this way, the hymn tells us very nearly the good news according to Matthew: Jesus was born to be the Messiah of Israel.

Most Christians probably do not need the Hebrew words *Emmanuel* and *Israel* translated. These words are familiar to us from our Bible studies, sermons, and Christmas plays. Matthew even translates the name for his readers: "'they will call him Immanuel' (which means 'God with us')" (Matt. 1:23).

This hymn (and Matthew's use of Isa. 7:14) is so familiar to us from Christmas that we rarely question it. But several questions must be asked: why is Jesus here, and only here, called Immanuel? What did Isaiah 7:14 mean in the centuries before it was applied to Jesus? And perhaps most important, What is it about Immanuel that is cause for Israel to be glad?

These questions are complicated because any honest answer to them must acknowledge that the Christian story does not begin with Christ. Almost nothing in our story makes sense without first borrowing the stories of Israel. The hymn tells us that Israel "mourns in lonely exile" and waits for the "key of David." Listen for Israel's exodus narrative in this stanza:

> O come, Adonai, Lord of might,
> Who to Thy tribes, on Sinai's height,
> In ancient times didst give the law
> In cloud and majesty and awe.
> Rejoice! Rejoice! Emmanuel
> Shall come to thee, O Israel.

If this is a Christian story, it is ours only to the extent that we have borrowed it. Let me take a moment to reiterate that this is my favorite Christmas song. I also, unabashedly, love Christmas. So I have something invested here: I want to claim this story as my own because it is the story that makes sense of Matthew's good news.[5] Even more, I want my students to recognize that Matthew is repurposing the exodus narrative to cast Jesus as a Moses figure. If I want to teach and preach about Christmas, I must borrow from another culture. This is something close to trespassing a cultural border without permission. Racial theorists might call this "cultural appropriation."

Cultural appropriation is a category of contemporary racial studies. It is "when members of one culture (call them outsiders for the sake of brevity) represent members of other cultures (insiders for the sake of convenience) or aspects of insiders' culture."[6] To be fair to my own insiders, it must be said that if I have benefited from appropriation, the cultural trespass was committed more than two thousand years ago. It is not completely clear, moreover, if a first-century author should be judged by contemporary racial ethics. What is clear to me is that, unlike the first followers of Jesus, I am not Jewish. It seems right then to acknowledge the debt I owe to Judaism during Advent. It also seems appropriate to wonder whether modern Christmas festivity gives our religious neighbors any cause to rejoice.

Advent, for this reason, seems like the least appropriate time to use Matthew's story as a religious wedge between neighbors. For Christians who observe Advent, the "Christmas season" is not a haphazard and vaguely demarcated whirlwind from Black Friday to New Year's.[7] Part of the reason that I take Advent seriously is that I do not want my calendar to be dominated by consumerism. For this reason I think that a return to the tradition of Advent may give us some perspective on the so-called war on Christmas.

Advent is a time for remembering and anticipating; it is *not* a time for proclaiming. Even less appropriate is the practice of proclaiming "Merry Christmas" during Advent and then crying "war" when others take issue with it. I can think of nothing less appropriate than using the Christian calendar as a battleground for a so-called war on Christmas whereby Christians jockey for cultural entitlement. If our Jewish neighbors prefer not to be greeted with "Merry Christmas," isn't this the least we could do to express our gratitude? And maybe more important, is not the hospitality of sojourners at the heart of the Christmas story?

Always Christmas

As I write this chapter it is November 10, 2015. You may remember it. It was the day that social media exploded with the news that Starbucks' coffee cups ruined Christmas. It seems that the paper cups at Starbucks are red and green today, but without any festive symbol or statement of "Merry Christmas." In the absence of a snowflake or a nativity star, Starbucks seems to be supporting

> Advent is a time for remembering and anticipating; it is not a time for proclaiming.

the war on Christmas—or at least this is what Lea Gabrielle of FOX News would have me believe. She introduced the topic like this: "The war on Christmas is off to an early start. Outrage is brewing across the country as Starbucks unveils holiday cups with no Christmas designs. And malls set up Santa shops with no trees or sleighs. Kelly Wright is here live with the backlash. Kelly, what are we seeing this morning?"[8]

The apparent lack of holiday cheer on these disposable cups attracted so much attention that the topic was addressed by presidential candidate Donald Trump. "If I become president we're all going to be saying 'Merry Christmas' again. That I can tell you."[9] Trump's statement was met by raucous cheers from his audience. Donald Trump (one hopes) is nothing more than a passing demagogue. But the so-called war on Christmas seems to find renewed vigor every year just prior to Thanksgiving. This controversy has been a media-generated discussion for over a decade now in America. Mark Pinsky's book *A Jew among the Evangelicals* testifies that the so-called war was already underway in 2005. Pinsky, a reporter for the *Orlando Sentinel*, writes, "The controversy over the largely imaginary 'War on Christmas' reached near-hysteria as the season drew near in 2005, fanned almost entirely by the cable news networks, including calls for boycotts of retail chains wishing customers 'Happy Holidays.'[10]

Pinsky rightly observes that cable news networks generate much of the debate. He labels the controversy "largely imagined." I would agree insomuch as most "culture wars" in America are perceptions creating conflicting realities.

The gist of the argument in favor of the reality of this "culture war" is that (1) liberals are conspiring to turn Christ into a dirty word, (2) most people celebrate Christmas, so who are we really offending anyway? and (3) we Christians ought to express our religious liberty by proclaiming our joy as an act of protest. As a Christian who celebrates Christmas, who does indeed say "Merry Christmas," and who partakes in the Who hash and the rare Who roast beast with great pleasure, allow me to assess this argument.

First, most Christians I know are not thrilled with what our culture has made of Christmas. C. S. Lewis wrote of his revulsion for the commercialization of "Xmas" in several personal letters. Once, when asked about his view on the holiday, he wrote:

> Three things go by the name of Christmas. One is a religious festival. This is important and obligatory for Christians; but as it can be of no interest to anyone else, I shall naturally say no more of it here. The second . . . is a popular holiday, an occasion for merrymaking and hospitality. If it were my business to have a "view" on this, I should say that I much approve of merrymaking. But what I approve of much more

is everybody minding his own business. I see no reason why I should volunteer views as to how other people should spend their own money in their own leisure among their own friends. It is highly probable that they want my advice on such matters as much as I want theirs. But the third thing called Christmas is unfortunately everyone's business. I mean of course the commercial racket. The interchange of presents was a very small ingredient in the older English festivity. . . . The idea that not only all friends but even all acquaintances should give one another presents, or at least send one another cards, is quite modern.

Lewis continues with what could be his most impassioned rant, using words like pain, overcrowded shops, illness, blackmail, Mrs. Busy, gaudy and useless fool, rubbish. He concludes, "It is in fact merely one annual symptom of that lunatic condition in our country, and indeed of the world, in which everyone lives by persuading everyone else to buy things. I don't know the way out."[11]

It takes very little imagination to guess what Lewis would think of Xmas in the new millennium. Not only do Christmas shoppers riot and trample each other at Walmart on Black Friday but the season is now at least two full months of consumerism. As an American, I contribute my disgust of witnessing this drive overshadow Thanksgiving. Comedian Jon Stewart asks, "There's a war on Christmas? Has anyone told Thanksgiving? 'Cause this year, Black Friday, a.k.a. Christmas's opening bell, got moved back a day to Black Thursday, or as we used to call it, Thanksgiving. Christmas is so big now, it's eating other holidays."[12]

It gets worse. Stewart joked about the eclipse of Thanksgiving in 2014. Only a year later, measuring by Donald Trump's indictment of Starbucks, the expectation of Christmas-themed products began in 2015 as early as November 10.

Lewis's vision for exile was a land of "always winter but never Christmas." In the world of Narnia, this was something of a childhood lament. In 2016, we are inching toward something even scarier: always Christmas, even when it's Halloween. Heeding the concerns of both Lewis and Stewart, we might consider the possibility that Christmas may indeed need saving. If so, the solution is not more Christmas-themed merchandise, but much, much less of it.

The second assumption in the war on Christmas argument is that the vast majority of Americans celebrate Christmas. As such, why worry—so goes the logic—about the minority of folks who do not? It is true that many more people celebrate Christmas than otherwise (at least in the four countries where I've lived). But I would suggest that Christians ought to care about the shadows we cast, whether they fall on a majority or minority of our neighbors. The argument could be made that we should care especially about our impact on minorities. Jesus commanded care for the "least of these," not the "most of these."

Speaking from personal experience, most of my friends who do not celebrate Christmas are not much offended by the phrase Merry Christmas. What is problematic is when Christians celebrate Christmas without any gesture of respect for their neighbors. For example, Larry Behrendt moderates a blog for Jewish-Christian dialogue. Behrendt writes, "If you want to greet me with a 'Merry Christmas,' I'm fine with that. But what is *wrong* with the alternative 'Happy Holiday' greeting that says, 'I don't know what holiday you celebrate this time of year, but whatever holiday it is, I hope you enjoy it.'"

> I would suggest that Christians ought to care about the shadows we cast, whether they fall on a majority or minority of our neighbors.

When said from a posture of peace on earth and goodwill toward all humanity, most non-Christians I know are quite happy to be happy for us as we celebrate. Like almost anything, much more is deemed acceptable within the context of friendship. What is especially vexing to "outsiders" is when Christians deck the halls of every public space available for decking and then complain that they are being targeted for religious persecution. From Behrendt's perspective, it seems like "every mall and town square is decorated for Christmas" and "the media is saturated with Christmas advertising, Christmas-themed programming, and [Christmas music]." He asks, "What holiday is celebrated in the West with more enthusiasm, with more stamina and more publicly than Christmas?"[13]

But some Christians see a greater threat at work. Franklin Graham explains that "the war on Christmas isn't really about Christmas at all—it's about the Son of God. The war on Christmas is a war on Christ and His followers. It's the hatred of our culture for the exclusive claims that Christ made."[14] Behrendt responds to Graham's war language from a Jewish perspective. He is careful to speak for himself only. Even so, I imagine that he echoes many of the neighbors of Christianity:

> This is where I feel compelled to say something, from the vantage point of Jewish-Christian dialogue. I will not comment on whether "Christ and His followers" are under attack in the United States, Canada, the U.K. or anywhere else. I will say simply that talk like this strikes most Jews as paranoid nonsense. *We don't get it.* From our perspective, it is close to inconceivable that any group could be safer, more secure from attack and more privileged than American Christians. From our perspective, a "war" on a religion does not look like a dispute over where Christmas carols might be sung, and

discussion of where a religious display may be placed does not amount to "hatred" of a religious culture. For Jews, a "war" on religion looks like Kristallnacht, and "hatred" of a religious culture looks like Auschwitz. If you think that Christmas is under attack and you want me to understand your point of view, try to remember that there's persecution and there's PERSECUTION. I mean, I doubt that the Christians of Egypt or the Sudan think that there's a "war" on Christmas in America.

In my process of learning about Christians and Christianity, I've learned that some Christians do sometimes feel marginalized and put on the defensive, particularly in places like college campuses. I don't pretend to understand this experience, and I do hope that Christians will take the time to explain their experience to me (hopefully in ways less hyperbolic than proclaiming that someone has declared "war" on them). But I do not presume to tell Christians what they should think or how they should feel. If "Happy Holidays" bugs you, then it bugs you.

You're entitled to prefer "Merry Christmas" to "Happy Holidays." By the same logic, you're entitled to prefer "Happy Holidays" to "Merry Christmas." All I'm asking for is a little charity. If I wish you "Happy Holidays," it's not because (as Franklin Graham put it) I intend to treat Jesus in a "scandalously secular way that denies His deity and saving work." I'm just trying to negotiate my way through a complex multicultural world. Ideally, those who feel that their Christianity is under attack can find a way to communicate that feeling in a way that people like me can understand. But at minimum, I ask that I not be demonized as I fumble for the right form of Season's Greeting.[15]

I do not agree with everything Behrendt writes here. For example, the phrase "Happy Holidays" is no solution. This phrase lacks sensitivity to the eight million Jehovah's Witnesses who do not observe holidays as a rule. (I admire their devotion to this rule and often wish that I could do likewise.) Simply adopting a vague gesture does little to help and probably exacerbates the existing problems. The best solution will not be found in a more tolerant slogan. The best—and perhaps only solution—is to get to know and care for our neighbors no matter what we say.

On my street in Dayton, there are several religious traditions represented. Among my most immediate neighbors are Muslims, Mormons, Jehovah's Witnesses, Jews, and Baptists. Our houses are a stone's throw from each other and so, of course, throwing stones is not an option. Christmas cookies are better than stones. But cookies that demonstrate a bit of sensitivity to my neighbors who do not celebrate Christmas are the best of all options.

The greater trouble, as Lewis notes, is the saturated commercialization that is either shared or witnessed by the general public. If I know that my neighbor feels alienated by Christmas cookies, the solution is simple. But public spaces, advertising, and Christmas-themed programming is designed to be impersonal. One can "mind his own business" as Lewis says and not be much offended if yours is the dominant culture. But as a minority during November and December, it is more difficult to mind your own business when Big Business ensures that you are reminded of Christmas every time you turn on the radio, check social media, or drive to the grocery store. And this is where understanding our religious neighbors (generally speaking) is important even if they are strangers.

Christmas is complicated. We don't want it to be complicated, but it is. Many Christians look around and see consumerism, decorated trees, Santa Clauses, elves, and snowmen. We see these everywhere and think none of these symbols relate to our faith. These symbols are not part of the Christian narrative. "Let It

Snow!"—just to name one song—has nothing to do with the nativity of Christ. So what is especially Christian about this song? We see these commercialized symbols as a nod to the secular. Some of us side with Lewis; we are offended by the unabashed drive to monetize our sacred calendar.

Whereas many non-Christians see these as clear symbols of Christianity. Jon Stewart, for example, perceives Black Friday as "Christmas's opening bell." In this case, many Christians and Jews witness the same drive to monetize and saturate November and interpret it differently.

Some of us side with Lewis; we are offended by the unabashed drive to monetize our sacred calendar.

The divergence in perceptions becomes clear only once we become sensitive to the "other." I suggest that we stop and take interest in *why* others see the world differently than we do. Not only will we understand and appreciate our neighbors better, we will understand ourselves better in the process.

This is where the topic gets personal for me. Christmas is a story of divine intervention. For the Christian, the incarnation of Christ is one of *the* great moments of divine intervention. It is the part of the story where God gets most personal. Because of this, Christmas can be the time of year when God's silence is the most potent. For those of us who do not often experience divine intervention on a personal level, the story of the incarnation can be alienating. Still, I hope. I happily suspend my disbelief to prepare myself for worship. But the Christmas-themed consumerism is almost deafening. It makes listening for God's voice all the more difficult.

Christmas and Social Power

Matthew's story of Jesus' birth continues to fascinate me. It is stunning in several ways, but I am struck again and again by how bizarre it all seems. My list of questions grows with every reading. Why must Mary be impregnated? Why is this accomplished in such a strange way? How does a Spirit sire flesh and blood? Do the dreams of Joseph point to the dreaming Joseph of Genesis? How does the birth of Jesus fulfill the prophecy expecting a baby named Immanuel? Why is it that magi (or experts in foreign magic) recognize Jesus' significance when no wise men in Israel enter the narrative? What does astrology have to do with Israel's Messiah? These are just a few of my questions, and no amount of study satisfies my curiosity.

The most interesting element of the plot is the characterization of Herod: Herod, *the absurdly powerless king*. Historically speaking, Herod governed Israel by Roman authority for almost forty years. He was a shrewd politician and a prolific builder. He built a temple in Jerusalem that trumped Solomon's in grandeur. Some ancient sources call him a madman. But you do not enjoy so much longevity in such a precarious political environment without being self-aware and calculating and having a store of political capital. Yet, according to Matthew's portrait, Herod seems almost inept. He is insecure, fooled by astrologers, ill-tempered, and given to overreaction. If not for the grotesque slaughter of children, we might almost think of him as a clown. Perhaps Matthew is offering us a political parody.

In my view, Matthew is creatively shaming Herod by revealing the truth about him. As a point of historical fact (not mentioned in the New Testament), Herod claimed to be a descendant of David by fabricating a genealogy. He was not the first to do this, but his false claim to the throne made many suspicious of him. Or perhaps widespread suspicions gave Herod the idea to create a false genealogy. Whatever the case, a council of Jewish leaders openly condemned him during his reign. Matthew seems to hold a similar opinion. Pushing this political agenda further, Matthew uses Herod as a foil to reveal something true about Jesus. A new "son of David" has arrived, and he is not appointed by Rome. This "son" is endorsed by heaven.

To make this point, Matthew crafts a parody. Matthew builds from a fundamental truth: responsible power does not act as Herod acts. This is where Matthew is simultaneously most creative and most true: the God of Jewish testimony is more likely to elevate an infant than endorse a king like Herod.

In these first few pages of the New Testament, we learn that the first Christmas was about power dynamics. The truth of the good news is tied to a political commentary: God is revealed in the powerless, revamping political systems and reversing fortunes. Of course, the revealing of the divine demonstrates a different kind of power. We eventually learn that Jesus has a kind of power that Herod does not demonstrate in this story. Or, put another way, Herod does not exhibit the kind of power that really matters in God's economy.

Luke's infancy narrative is much different in several respects. Herod is mentioned, but Luke does not weave Herod's story into the plot until Jesus is an adult. What Luke and Matthew have in common, however, is an interest in power reversals. Luke at times is even more direct with this theme. Consider the song that Mary sings before she gives birth to Jesus:

> The truth of the good news is tied to a political commentary: God is revealed in the powerless, revamping political systems and reversing fortunes.

My soul glorifies the Lord
    and my spirit rejoices in God my Savior,
for he has been mindful
    of the humble state of his servant.

From now on all generations will call me blessed,
> for the Mighty One has done great things for me—
>> holy is his name.
His mercy extends to those who fear him,
> from generation to generation.
He has performed mighty deeds with his arm;
> he has scattered those who are proud in their inmost
>> thoughts.
He has brought down rulers from their thrones
> but has lifted up the humble.
He has filled the hungry with good things
> but has sent the rich away empty.
He has helped his servant Israel,
> remembering to be merciful
to Abraham and his descendants forever,
> just as he promised our ancestors.

—LUKE 1:46–55

Mary sings these words acknowledging her "humble state." She sings of the reversal of fortunes. The proud are scattered; rulers are ousted; the rich are emptied. Clearly those who derive power from prestige, high office, or wealth are humiliated. Conversely, the humble are elevated.

Matthew has magi; Luke has shepherds. Matthew has a star; Luke has an angelic host. Matthew tells of a flight to Egypt; Luke tells of a visit to Elizabeth's house. The two Christmas stories are dramatically different! One of the few things that the Christmas stories of Matthew and Luke have in common is a clear message: *if you* occupy a place of power when Jesus arrives, you are likely to lose it in humiliating fashion. Both Gospels remind us that this is exactly the sort of thing that the God of Israel is known to do.

Christians who follow the church calendar get an opportunity to participate in these stories every year. We get to sing along-side Mary and ponder in our hearts the most unlikely manner of divine intervention. These stories are told and retold so that the vulnerability of our almighty God will trouble us and ultimately win us over. We get a chance to puzzle over the paradox of a God who chooses to sire a mortal son. We are invited to humble our-selves and wait for God to do something absurd and miraculous. At the very least we tell these stories each year to remind ourselves what sort of God we worship.

The danger of commemorating this narrative every year is that it can become commonplace. Those of us who celebrate it come to expect the incarnation as if it were owed to us. Many Christians in America act like we own the months of November and December. A time of year that is meant to commemorate the most unexpected gift can easily become a season of insufferable entitlement. Because of the social power American Christians have, we begin to defend that to which we feel entitled. Somewhere along this path from unexpected grace to false entitlement, we have lost something sacred. An ancient story meant to challenge entrenched social powers is ironically defended by entrenched social powers in modern America.

Unexpected Grace

Peter, Susan, and Lucy are on the run. Edmond has chased the White Witch in search of Turkish delight, and so he is not with the rest of the children. The reader will remember Edmond's peril and the sound of the witch's sleigh. She is the one who rides on a sledge drawn by two reindeer. The sound of jingling announces her arrival because her reindeer have harnesses of scarlet leather covered in bells. She has turned Mr. Tumnus to stone, and she holds Narnia under a curse: always winter and never Christmas.

It is then only natural for the young reader to feel Lucy's fear at the sound of bells:

> It seemed to Lucy only the next minute (though really it was hours and hours later) when she woke up feeling a little cold and dreadfully stiff and thinking how she would like a hot bath. Then she felt a set of long whiskers tickling her cheek and saw the cold daylight coming in through the mouth of the cave. But immediately after that she was very wide awake indeed, and so was everyone else. In fact they were all sitting up with their mouths and eyes wide open listening to a sound which was the very sound they'd all been thinking of (and sometimes imagining they heard) during their walk last night. It was a sound of jingling bells.

Lucy—and the reader with her—expects the sound of bells to mean doom. Mr. Beaver, instead, delivers good news. "'Didn't I tell you,' answered Mr. Beaver, 'that she'd made it always winter and never Christmas? Didn't I tell you? Well, just come and see!'"

Then the children meet the person they least expect: Father Christmas. When my children were reading this book with me, I asked, "Do you know who Father Christmas is?" Even though we never called St. Nicholas by this name in our house, they were both certain that it was Santa. True to form, Father Christmas brings gifts. Unexpectedly, and true only within *The Lion, the Witch and the Wardrobe*, Father Christmas signals an end to the witch's magic. Or (if you are like me and read this story for merging mythologies) Father Christmas anticipates the end of exile and oppression. "'Locks and bolts make no difference to me,' said Father Christmas."[16] His arrival marks the liberation from Narnia's long winter.

This story, like every good Christmas story, contains an

unexpected gift. The children, of course, receive gifts. But the greater gift is a literary irony: when almost certain doom is anticipated by jingling bells, an equally grandiose but opposite character arrives. The reader is taken from dread to hope in the process.[17] This unexpected turn is the gift. Moreover, it is a gift only because it is unexpected.

Now I come to my point. The children in this story are not *asking* for presents. They have written no letters to Santa. They—along with the young reader—are unaware that Father Christmas even belongs to this story. Lucy is a refugee hoping to escape and survive. She is stranger in a strange land and under no illusion of entitlement. The gift (*charis* means both gift and grace in Greek) is not an entitlement. Doesn't this make the arrival of Christmas all the sweeter?

The trouble with what Lewis called "Xmas" is that too many of us feel entitled to it. And if we feel entitled to Christmas, don't we rob it of its most gracious virtue? Isn't a sense of entitlement fundamentally opposite to a sense of grace? I am of the opinion that the appreciation of grace requires the experience of an unexpected turn.

> Lucy is a refugee hoping to escape and survive. She is stranger in a strange land and under no illusion of entitlement.

Of course, those who celebrate Advent (and I would recommend this over a culture war) can hardly meet Christmas unexpectedly. Advent is about remembering and anticipating, after all. We can, however, anticipate without a sense of entitlement. My guess is that this will make Christmastime more enjoyable for our neighbors and for us.

CHAPTER 3

On the Border of Jesus and Genocide

> If ever the book which I am not going to write is written it must be the full confession by Christendom of Christendom's specific contribution to the sum of human cruelty and treachery. Large areas of "the World" will not hear us till we have publicly disowned much of our past.
>
> —C. S. LEWIS, *THE FOUR LOVES*

> Ask a mixed group of Christians and Jews, "What does the Cross mean to you?" Christians may say that it signals Christ's incomparable gift of his life so that they might be saved; Jews may counter that it symbolizes unspeakable terror.
>
> —RABBI MICHAEL COOK

A Legacy of Mass Murder

Nobody wants to talk about the Holocaust. It may well be the most repulsive topic there is and there is no way to approach it that avoids offense. It is rendered all the more offensive on the lips of those of us who cannot imagine this catastrophe, much less make sense of it. Worse, this genocide meets us in the present as we continue to feel its impact in countless ways. It is equally true that we—Christians especially—must discuss the Holocaust.[1] There are a number of reasons for this, including the necessity to avoid tendencies that create cultures of mass murder.

History is replete with examples of Christians who attempted to "solve" social problems with mass murder. I did not always believe this. In my youth when I heard such accusations I assumed that no Christian could commit such a crime and still qualify as a Christian. Or I thought that demagogues and despots often acted out of personal or political interests and used the religion of Christianity as a political tool. There are historical episodes that point to such interpretations. Conversely, there are many episodes in Christian history that show otherwise. Charlemagne, for example, created an office called the *Magister Judaeorum* (or "Master of the Jews"). This state-appointed officer served as an advocate for Jews in the Roman Empire who were being persecuted by Christians.[2] In this case, it was the politician who stood as a defense against the church's violence. Or consider this example: concurrent with the Ottoman Empire, many Jews fleeing from Christian persecution found safe haven among Muslims. I mention these examples because the Nazis who designed the "final solution" stood in the trajectory of centuries of theologically motivated anti-Judaism. I do not deny the many good things that Christians have done. Nor am I of the mind that Christianity necessarily breeds episodes of mass murder. Conversely, it is important to realize that Christianity has indeed bred a great many episodes of mass murder. The notion that a few bad apples are to blame for this legacy is simply no longer an option. We now know too much about the role of Christians and Christianity in the evolution of European anti-Semitism that culminated in the Holocaust. Christianity is as guilty of mass murder as any other political force.

Here I risk generalization, but examples are easy enough to find. Here are two: the Rhineland massacres of 1096, and the use of smallpox-infected blankets on indigenous people in North America. I mention these two specific examples to show the risk obscuring larger contexts. If I focus on the 1096 mass murder of Jews by Christians, I risk neglecting the larger story of the Crusades that spans centuries. If I focus on the smallpox episodes of American and Canadian colonial history, I risk neglecting the larger story of our systematic displacement and mass murder of hundreds of tribes. These are not isolated episodes of an otherwise positive Christian history. This is an important thread that runs throughout our history. It is a major theme, not a minor subplot. Worse, as hard as this is to hear, our mass murders have often been theologically motivated. When Christians have approved of mass murder, many—far too many—believed that God was on their side or that it was for the greater good and that God would soon forgive. In our history, much of Christian violence against Jews has been theologically motivated by the belief that all Jews of all times are responsible for the death of Jesus.

> When Christians have approved of mass murder, many—far too many—believed that God was on their side or that it was for the greater good and that God would soon forgive.

The We-Our-Us Problem

What I am about to write is source of great shame for me, and I do so with the weight of knowing that anything I write will be inadequate. So I ask you to read the next paragraph with the strongest possible emphasis:

The vast majority of Christians forget our complicity. We repeatedly commemorate our virtuous episodes to cover up our appalling vices. American and "Allied" Christians are especially guilty of this as we fail to remember the role of Christians as passive and active perpetrators of the Holocaust.

One of the major reasons that American Christians in

particular avoid accepting blame is that "we" fought against Germany. The Nazis killed many of "our" soldiers. Indeed many of "us" were targeted by Axis forces. I call this the "we-our-us" problem. In our collective memories, heroic figures of the past remain part of "us." Ignoble figures of the past are often distanced as "them."

Allow me to use a different historical episode to illustrate the problem. I grew up a Californian of European lineage. Early "pilgrims" in California (Spanish missionaries, Russian settlers, gold-seeking forty-niners, railroad builders, etc.) sounded the death knell for indigenous tribes. More than 90 percent of indigenous peoples in California were scattered and killed from 1800 to 1900. European-born epidemics, invasive plant life, tribal displacement, and physical violence proved fatal on a massive scale. As a Californian, are *my* people to blame? If I focus on my specific ancestors, I might avoid this association to some extent. My people—the Italians—were not the perpetrators of these particular crimes. We were dealing with our own difficulties elsewhere. Italians were not yet considered white at this point in American history, and my family members were not yet established in California anyway.

> In our collective memories, heroic figures of the past remain part of "us." Ignoble figures of the past are often distanced as "them."

Now to the bigger picture. There are three reasons why this version of my family history does not alleviate my people from blame: (1) I am an American, and native genocide is an American problem; (2) my family benefited from the violence done to native populations as we eventually became land owners; (3) I am a Christian first and foremost, and my identity in Christ is most important. So "my people" must include Americans at large,

Californian colonists, and, most important, Christians past, present, and future.

So too with the Holocaust. For better or worse, my imperfections belong to the church, and the many imperfections of the church belong to me. While legacy is often a matter of choosing which cultural memories to commemorate, certain legacies follow us even (perhaps especially) when we try to wish them away. It would be inappropriate for me to disassociate myself from this tragic legacy.

I am convinced that many Christians (especially American Christians) disassociate themselves from the legacy of the Holocaust because we have constructed a heroic "we-our-us" in our history of World War II. In our popular narratives, all of the war crimes were committed by an evil "them" group. But if there were Christians among the perpetrators, if Christian anti-Semitism is in any way related, the Holocaust becomes no longer simply a Nazi problem; it becomes a "we-our-us" problem. What do we make of the fact that there was a Nazi branch of the Protestant church before and during these years?[3] What do we make of the bishops who openly supported Nazism or the Christian chaplains who actively supported the officers of the death camps? And to the larger question: if it is not a "few" Christians, or even "many" Christians, but an entire legacy of Christians justifying mass murder theologically, what does this say about Christian theology?

Memory and Identity

A survey conducted by the Pew Research Center aimed to explore Jewish identity by asking, "What does being Jewish mean in America today?" The study found that "large majorities of U.S. Jews say that remembering the Holocaust (73 percent) and leading an ethical life (69 percent) are essential to their sense of

Jewishness."[4] Other major factors contributing to American Jewishness included "working for justice and equality," "caring about Israel," and "a good sense of humor." This survey suggests that for most American Jews remembering the Holocaust is the first and most important element of Jewishness. Anecdotally, I know that many of my Jewish friends are uncomfortable with this identity marker and would like to change it if they could.

Memory—both for individuals and groups—is identity forming. In this case especially, remembrance is not a simple act of looking back; it is a defining factor in the present. Jewish identity as it relates to the Holocaust is evolving as memories of it take new life in second and third generations. But the importance of the memory remains strong. At the risk of absurd understatement, most Christians do not have the same existential connection with Holocaust memories. For Christians—even Christians who are keenly interested—we lack the ability to experience the Holocaust as a family history. Our collective interest has passed into the realm of textbooks, documentaries, occasional museum visits, and chapters like the one before you now. Whereas Holocaust remembrance is first on the list for American Jews, it probably would not make the top one hundred list of Christian identity markers. This is just another way of saying that the Holocaust is not a factor in Christian self-definition.

It should not surprise us, then, that the question of Christian complicity is complicated when Jews and Christians compare their histories. I have learned that Jews and Christians tend to measure Christian complicity differently. And of course there are likely as many different Jewish perspectives on this topic as there are ways of forgetting it among Christians. In preparing this chapter for publication, two Jewish friends (both senior colleagues) suggested that Christian complicity should not be overstated. So

I acknowledge that there is danger in overstating Christian complicity and the general perception of this complicity among Jews. But I am convinced that understatement risks more. Most of my research on this topic has echoed something similar to this summary: "Modern antisemitism's thorough dehumanization of the Jews, which facilitated their mass murder, drew upon centuries of theologically encouraged disdain."[5]

Not only do most American Jews feel in some way personally connected to Holocaust memory, many Jewish scholars associate Christianity with the problem. Simply put, (a) European anti-Semitism fit hand in glove with Christianity for more than a millennium; (b) such ideology made the Holocaust possible. I would also suggest that most Christians do not know this. We Christians, by comparison, know very little about the Holocaust and know even less how important remembering it is to our Jewish neighbors. The implication here should be clear: *we* don't know the first thing about Jews.

> Simply put, (a) European anti-Semitism fit hand in glove with Christianity for more than a millennium; (b) such ideology made the Holocaust possible.

From Jesus to Hitler in a Single Breath

I have found that the most pressing question that evangelical Christians have about Jews is this: why don't they accept Jesus as the Messiah?[6] There is a good answer to this, but I will not give it here. Instead I will point out that this is the wrong question. Of course, no question should be wrong in Jewish-Christian dialogue. It becomes wrong only when it becomes the most important question to the Christian. It is wrong if it assumes that Jesus is the most significant border between us. The better question—the one that ought to be most pressing for Christians—is one that we must ask ourselves: to what extent is Christianity responsible for the Holocaust?

When I first heard this question, it scandalized me. I thought that surely many *Christians* were complicit. Anti-Semites masquerading as Christians should get their share of the blame. But Christianity itself is not to blame! Christians—those who got Christianity all wrong—are the problem. This was my kneejerk reaction and I imagine that many Christians will feel the same if faced with this question. The truth is more problematic and is not revealed properly unless it is discovered in Jewish-Christian conversation.

Here is an excerpt of a recent conversation I had with my friend Larry Behrendt.[7] Larry is the son of a Jewish German who left the country shortly before the death camps were heavily populated. (In this dialogue Larry and I use the word *Shoah,* which is Hebrew for "catastrophe" and emphasizes the singular nature of the Holocaust.)

ANTHONY: I feel like we're at a certain moment where the climate is right for ideological shifts, and it seems like for whatever reason there are more Jews and Christians willing to have conversations. I don't know if there are more participants than in any time in history, but it seems like there's a lot more than there were in many other times in history.

LARRY: This is the best time in history for me to write my blog. If I tried to write this blog in the thirteenth century, it never would've gotten off the ground.[8]

ANTHONY: So for me, it's crucial that we take the opportunity to compare narratives. And I think, at least from the Christian side, I've found that Christians are actually quite appalled at the amount of damage that

Christianity has done. They know very vaguely about the Crusades . . .

LARRY: And you believe that the Crusades are now viewed in Christianity as a negative thing.

ANTHONY: (laughing) Oh, absolutely.

LARRY: It was not a heroic effort to wrestle the Holy Land from the infidel?

ANTHONY: No, no.

LARRY: Okay. What if I were to say that Christianity was solely responsible for the Shoah? I don't believe that today, but there was probably a time in my life when I did believe it.

ANTHONY: Now we're getting somewhere. I'm assuming that there are other Jews in the world that might say that very thing?

LARRY: Yes.

ANTHONY: If there are Jews who would say, "Christianity is solely responsible for the Shoah," and most Christians think that Christianity was in *no way* responsible for the Shoah, this is an enormous obstacle for Jewish-Christian dialogue . . .

LARRY: That's why this subject has to be on the table.

ANTHONY: . . . that will only be solved if we talk about it together.

LARRY: Before we get to that position—

ANTHONY: I'm already there. But go ahead anyway.

LARRY: Is the statement "I consider Christianity to be responsible for the Shoah" offensive to you?

ANTHONY: (sighs) It's not offensive to me. I don't think it tells the whole story, but I understand why someone might say that. In fact, I've gone so far as to say, "Luther is just as responsible as Hitler." I've said that in the past. And I've been shouted down by Christians for offering that narrative. . . . Let me try to answer your question about Christian complicity. It has to be a really complicated answer. It depends on when you want to begin the discussion. I have no problem with saying the New Testament itself has been used as a bludgeon in very real ways to do violence to the Jewish people. I am absolutely certain that this is not what Jesus had in mind, or what Paul had in mind, but it is the way their words have been co-opted. The world that Christianity created in Europe was hostile to Jews, often producing violence against Jews in an attempt to convert or kill. The extent to which Christianity is responsible for the Holocaust is unbelievable. I don't think Hitler was a Christian, but I think that Christianity alongside ten other factors—like race theory, and Nietzschean master-slave morality—combined to produce the Shoah.

LARRY: I want to throw two pieces of nuance onto your answer, one that exacerbates Christian responsibility, and one that alleviates it to some extent. The exacerbating factor is I don't think there needs to be a single Christian in Europe for Christianity to have a substantial responsibility for the Shoah. It is simply a cultural legacy.

ANTHONY: I would agree with that. Even if we were to say that every Nazi gave up their Christianity—

LARRY: And renounced it—

ANTHONY:—Christianity would still be in large part responsible for the Shoah. I would agree with that.

LARRY: It's one of the reasons why I want to move away from the question of the responsibility of Christians for the Shoah, and towards the question of the responsibility of Christianity. But there's a second factor here that I think we have to recognize: if we are looking at where we stand today, if we're looking at the recent thirty to fifty years of Jewish-Christian relations, at the academic push to understand the Jewish Jesus, I have to believe that the primary impetus for this golden age of Jewish-Christian relations is the Shoah. I am trying to figure out, why?

Here Larry and I are assuming a distinction between Christians (real-world people who act for better or worse in particular ways) and Christianity (the system of theological ideas and cultural practices). Of course, the two cannot be so neatly separated. But—and this is key—neither can we separate the religion and politics of anti-Semitism. It will simply not do to blame particular Christians for the many sins that led to the Holocaust. I do not doubt that there are many individuals who indeed deserve blame. But it must also be said that cultural systems and ideologies produced by Christianity have been devastating for our Jewish neighbors. The theology incorporated an anti-Jewish element very early on and created a legacy that must be acknowledged.

Famously, G. K. Chesterton wrote, "The Christian ideal has not been tried and found wanting. It has been found difficult; and left untried."[9] I like this. Chesterton was the kind of Christian who recognized the deep failings of Christians. From beyond Christian borders, both Gandhi and George Bernard Shaw make very similar observations about the nobility of Christian ideals. In Chesterton's testimony, there is an assumption that the invention of Christianity was pure, only corrupted by an imperfect people. But my point is different. Even many of our highest ideals and earliest traditions have been catastrophically bad for Jews and Judaism. Rabbi Michael Cook, a colleague of mine in New Testament studies, writes:

Etched even more deeply into the modern Jewish psyche was Nazism's exploitation of New Testament supersessionist theology. This conviction—that Gentile-Christians had displaced and replaced the Jews as God's chosen people—was manipulated by Hitler's ideologues to suggest that the persistence of Jews into the twentieth century was an anomaly, a quirk or mistake of history; Jews were a fossil meant to have disappeared far earlier. Such a ploy lessened potential resistance to Hitler's "Final Solution," the plan to exterminate the entire Jewish people. Jews today who do not believe that the New Testament itself caused the Holocaust will likely yet insist that the Holocaust could not have occurred without it."[10]

Cook has his finger on the difference between how Jewish memory (in large part) and Christian memory (in large part) differ. He also suggests that several passages in the New Testament are now linked with the Holocaust. Most Christians rightly place the New Testament as a central identity marker of our faith. Yet the New Testament is also positioned at a particularly catastrophic Jewish-Christian border.

There is perhaps nothing that illustrates this point better than the history of Christian passion plays. Remembering the death and resurrection of Jesus is the most central element of Christian identity. With this in mind, the succinct explanation on the Anti-Defamation League (an organization that promotes Jewish well-being) webpage is worthy of a careful read:

> The central narrative of Christian theology is the passion, i.e. the trials and crucifixion, and resurrection of Jesus. . . . Good Friday and Easter celebrate respectively the crucifixion and resurrection of Jesus as the high points of Christian creed and experience. Christians frequently present dramatic

representations of this narrative known as "passion plays." . . . Historically, Holy Week (the week leading up to Easter Sunday) was a period when Jews were most vulnerable and when Christians perpetrated some of the worst violence against their Jewish neighbors.[11]

Christianity Today writer Collin Hansen helpfully explains "why some Jews fear The Passion" in conversation with Abraham Foxman. Hansen reminds us that "during and immediately following the Middle Ages, enraged passion play spectators sometimes invaded the ghettos to exact revenge on Jews for killing Jesus." Many Jews have not forgotten the outcomes of such passion plays. Foxman reminds us, "For almost 2,000 years in Western civilization, four words legitimized, rationalized, and fueled anti-Semitism: 'The Jews killed Christ.'" What Hansen writes next will be jarring to hear for most Christians: "When Foxman envisions Christ's crucifixion, he does not think about love, forgiveness, or hope. He recalls the Holocaust and Hitler's chilling praise for the famed Oberammergau Passion Play in 1934."[12]

Now, you might ask, how did we get from Jesus to Hitler in a single breath? After attending the annual passion play in Oberammergau, Adolf Hitler offered his endorsement of the long-standing tradition: "It is vital that the Passion play be continued at Oberammergau; for never has the menace of Jewry been so convincingly portrayed as in this presentation of what happened in the time of the Romans."[13] Hitler then praised Pontius Pilate as an example of someone "racially and intellectually so superior" to Jews. According to Hitler, the Roman dignitary "stands out like a firm, clean rock in the middle of the whole muck and mire of Jewry." Oberammergau is only seventy miles from the Dachau concentration camp, established in 1933.[14]

If we distance the evils of Nazism too far from the Christian legacy of anti-Judaism, we risk the collective evil of repeating our anti-Jewish rhetoric without understanding the historic consequences of such rhetoric. European anti-Judaism is an opportune mirror for Western Christianity. Do we harbor some of the same inclinations to stereotype, to blame, to veil contempt with theological language? Do we ask questions about the theology of "the Jews" as if there is a groupthink shared by all Jews everywhere? Do we confuse the policies of the State of Israel with the sensibilities of the Jewish people? Do we teach our children to dislike the Pharisees in our Sunday schools and children's Bibles? Do we preach from John's Gospel without acknowledging the historic consequences of referring to "the Jews" as devils? Do we launch well-intentioned causes for the oppressed by comparing the traditionalists of today's church to the legalists of Paul's day? Do we explain the truth of Christianity as if it needs an opposite and outmoded counterpart?

These are all examples of our subtle inclinations. It is quite possible for Christian churches to exhibit all of these subtleties and still have warm feelings for our Jewish neighbors. I think that most American Christians do not know that they have inherited these germs of anti-Judaism. It is also possible that none of these theological positions will grow into overt contempt. Even so, the mirror provided by European anti-Judaism should at least suggest the possibility of infection. Words shape worlds. Christianity has demonstrated this fact time and again. With this in mind, we now must address the "we-our-us" problem of Martin Luther.

Terrible Little Books

The Christian church of my youth was woefully unaware of our history. We studied the Bible, not church history. We preferred the hymns of our grandparents to the creeds of the early church.

(The Independent Christian Churches consider themselves non-denominational.) The history of our movement was included in our weekly bulletin as a single paragraph. This short paragraph explained that the practices of Christianity began with the events recounted in the book of Acts and then were reinstated by Martin Luther. That was all there was to it. We were not Lutherans; most folks in our pews knew very little about Martin Luther. Even so, my little church and my young imagination placed Luther's name next to St. Paul's. There were no other luminaries of Christian history in our official literature.[15] Martin Luther loomed large as the singular, heroic Reformer.

In the autumn of 1997 I was researching for a church history class and I met a different side of Luther. I call this my "Luther concussion." The internet was young, but there were already enough online white supremacists to warrant a digital version of a little book by Martin Luther titled *The Jews and Their Lies*. Luther was not shy with his criticism of theological positions that differed from his own. He became famous for this very characteristic. It is also no secret that Jews and Christians have historically disagreed on Jesus' significance. Luther's theological arguments with Judaism are therefore not surprising. What is difficult to explain (as with all forms of anti-Semitism) is Luther's contempt for Jews in general.

In 1543 Luther offered advice to government officials. This advice was given so that, in his words, "we all can be rid of the unbearable, devilish burden of the Jews." Part of Luther's power was that he was a master at being memorable. Luther was not always as anti-Semitic as he seems in this book—or at least he does not appear to be. At times Luther appears to be quite friendly with "the brothers of our Lord." But nothing else Luther said about "the Jews" was nearly as influential. I cannot unread this book.

Luther's *The Jews and Their Lies* surfaced in my memory as I read another terribly memorable book: Elie Wiesel's *Night*. This book is Wiesel's autobiographical account of the Holocaust. I will set Luther's advice against Elie Wiesel's memories. I confess this is a copy-and-paste job that juxtaposes passages from both books. Perhaps I am being unjust to Luther's legacy.[16] The act of cutting and pasting rarely does justice to a great thinker's life or work. Luther is a world-shaping ideologue and his legacy is quite complex.[17] Even worse, I am truncating Wiesel's great work of literature, reducing it to mere fragments. There is no way to copy and paste from Wiesel's account of the Holocaust and do justice to its darkness.

I include it here because it is the only way that I can think of to convey the lasting effects of my Luther concussion. I cannot read Luther and not think of Wiesel; I cannot read Wiesel and not think of Luther. These two thin books—each influential—are fused in my mind. As you read, consider that Luther was writing to governmental officials in the 1542 and that Wiesel was writing of actions endorsed and commanded by government officials in the 1930s and '40s.

> I cannot read Luther and not think of Wiesel; I cannot read Wiesel and not think of Luther. These two thin books—each influential—are fused in my mind.

LUTHER: Therefore a Christian should be content and not argue with the Jews. But if you have to or want to talk with them, do not say any more than this: "Listen, Jew, are you aware that Jerusalem and your sovereignty, together with your temple and priesthood, have been destroyed for over 1,460 years?"[18]

WIESEL: During the day I studied the Talmud, and at night I ran to the synagogue to weep over the destruction of the Temple.[19]

LUTHER: In brief, dear princes and lords, those of you who have Jews under your rule—if my counsel does not please you, find better advice, so that you and we all can be rid of the unbearable, devilish burden of the Jews. . . . set fire to their synagogues or schools and to bury and cover with dirt whatever will not burn, so that no man will ever again see a stone or cinder of them. This is to be done in honor of our Lord and of Christendom, so that God might see that we are Christians, and do not condone or knowingly tolerate such public lying, cursing, and blaspheming of his Son and of his Christians.[20]

WIESEL: "The Jews in Budapest are living in an atmosphere of fear and terror. . . . The Fascists are attacking Jewish shops and synagogues."[21]

LUTHER: Second, I advise that their houses also be razed and destroyed. For they pursue in them the same aims as in their synagogues. Instead they might be lodged under a roof or in a barn, like the gypsies. This will bring home to them that they are not masters in our country, as they boast, but that they are living in exile and in captivity, as they incessantly wail and lament about us before God.[22]

WIESEL: The commandant announced that we had already covered forty-two miles since we left. . . . We sank down as one man in the snow. My father shook me. "Not here. . . . Get up. . . . A little farther on. There's a shed over there . . . come on."[23]

LUTHER: I advise that all their prayer books and Talmudic writings, in which such idolatry, lies, cursing and blasphemy are taught, be taken from them.[24]

WIESEL: It is obvious that the war which Hitler and his accomplices waged was a war not only against Jewish, men, women, and children, but also against Jewish religion, Jewish culture, Jewish tradition, therefore Jewish memory.[25]

LUTHER: I advise that their rabbis be forbidden to teach henceforth on pain of loss of life and limb.[26]

WIESEL: On the seventh day of Passover the curtain rose. The Germans arrested the leaders of the Jewish community.[27]

LUTHER: I advise that safe-conduct on the highways be abolished completely for the Jews.[28]

WIESEL: There are anti-Semitic incidents every day, in the streets, in the trains. . . . The situation is getting very serious.[29]

LUTHER: I advise that usury be prohibited to them, and that all cash and treasure of silver and gold be taken from them and put aside for safekeeping.[30]

WIESEL: A Jew no longer had the right to keep in his house gold, jewels, or any objects of value. Everything had to be handed over to the authorities—on pain of death. My father went down into the cellar and buried our savings.[31]

WIESEL: "Look, take this knife," he said to me. "I don't need it any longer. It might be useful to you. And take this spoon as well. Don't sell them. Quickly! Go on take what I'm giving you!" The inheritance. "Don't talk like that, father." (I felt that I would break into sobs.) "I don't want to hear you say that. Keep the spoon and the knife. You need them as much as I do. . . ." He looked at me with eyes that veiled despair.[32]

LUTHER: I commend putting a flail, an ax, a hoe, a spade, a distaff, or a spindle into the hands of young, strong Jews and Jewesses and letting them earn their bread in the sweat of their brow, as was imposed on the children of Adam.[33]

WIESEL: "Remember this," he went on. "Remember it forever. Engrave it into your minds. You are at Auschwitz. And Auschwitz is not a convalescent home. It's a concentration camp. Here, you have got to work. If not, you will go straight to the furnace. To the crematory. Work or the crematory—the choice is in your hands."[34]

LUTHER: Therefore be on your guard against the Jews, knowing that wherever they have their synagogues, nothing is found but a den of devils.[35]

LUTHER: Toss out these lazy rogues by the seat of their pants.[36]

WIESEL: Another time we had to load Diesel engines on to trains supervised by German soldiers. Idek's nerves were on edge. He was restraining himself with great difficulty. Suddenly, his frenzy broke out. The victim was my father. "You lazy old devil!" Idek began to yell. "Do you call that work?" And he began to beat him with an iron bar.[37]

LUTHER: I wish and I ask that our rulers who have Jewish subjects exercise a sharp mercy toward these wretched people, as suggested above, to see whether this might not help (though it is doubtful). They must act like a good physician who, when gangrene has set in, proceeds without mercy to cut, saw, and burn flesh, veins, bone, and marrow. Such a procedure must also be followed in this instance. Burn down their synagogues, forbid all that I enumerated earlier, force them to work, and deal harshly with them, as Moses did in the wilderness, slaying three thousand lest the whole people perish.[38]

WIESEL: The Jews were made to get out. They were made to dig huge graves. And when they were finished their work, the Gestapo began theirs. Without passion, without haste, they slaughtered their prisoners. Each one had to go to the hole and present his neck. Babies were thrown into the air and the machine gunners used them as targets.[39]

LUTHER: Let the government deal with them in this respect, as I have suggested.[40]

I do not know what Martin Luther would think if he knew that his advice would be carried out so literally and brutally. I would like to think that Luther would regret his words if he could foresee how they would be used. Maybe he would have recanted if he knew that the state religion of Germany would someday be called Lutheran and that many of the Christians who admired him would become genocidal. It is also possible that Luther would have approved. He did, after all, write those words for the purpose of governance.

Perhaps coincidentally, the worst pogrom (theologically motivated acts of destruction of Jewish property and violence against Jews) in history occurred on Martin Luther's birthday in 1938. Those who remember this date remember it as The Night of Broken Glass or *Kristallnacht*.[41] On November 9–10 of this year over seven thousand Jewish businesses were vandalized and looted, over two hundred synagogues were destroyed, and over thirty thousand Jews were sent to the camps at Buchenwald, Dachau, and Sachsenhausen. I wonder how many Christians were directly involved. Did they know where their hatred came from? Did Luther know where his came from?

CHAPTER 4

On the Border of Dogma and Underdogma

> The greatest evil . . . is conceived and ordered (moved, seconded, carried, and minuted) in clean, carpeted, warmed and well-lighted offices, by quiet men with white collars and cut fingernails and smooth-shaven cheeks who do not need to raise their voices.
>
> —C. S. LEWIS, PREFACE TO *THE SCREWTAPE LETTERS*

> As a Christian, I can, I must, and I ought always to have or to find a bridge to the Jew in my heart. But as a Christian, I also have to follow the laws of my Volk. . . . Even if I know that "thou shalt not kill" is a commandment of God, or that "thou shalt love the Jew" because he too is a child of the eternal Father, I am able to know as well that I have to kill him, I have to shoot him. And I can only do that if I am permitted to say: Christ.
>
> —SIEGFRIED LEFFLER, A 1936 SERMON

Christian Morality

Christians who have long stood in opposition to Nazi ideology will have problems—hopefully major problems—with the view that Christianity and Nazism are in some way compatible. In retrospect, for most Christians, Nazi ideology has become the very epitome of evil.[1] There is truth to the narrative that the Christians among the Allied forces fought for the better cause over and against the Christians among the Axis forces. Surely the clergy

99

who opposed Nazism were closer to the side of the angels. Surely the clergy (perhaps as many as 67 percent of the clergy in Axis countries) who allowed the ideology of Aryan superiority to infiltrate the church were not following the teachings of Jesus. But the narrative that tells us that the Christians were the "good guys" in those years is misleading.

It is probably true that most Christians today are not anti-Semitic. It is almost certainly true that most English-speaking Christians consider Nazism to be altogether evil. C. S. Lewis assumes as much in the first chapters of Mere Christianity. He writes, "Progress means not just changing, but changing for the better. If no set of moral ideas were truer or better than any other, there would be no sense in preferring civilised morality to savage morality, or Christian morality to Nazi morality."[2]

I will leave aside for the moment the distinction between "civilised morality" and "savage morality." Let us first remember that Lewis lived through the Nazi air raids. War has a tendency to entrench people in absolute categories of good and evil. Lewis refers to the Nazis often in the first chapters of Mere Christianity and for good reason. I do not fault him for setting Christian morality against Nazi morality.

I will also happily concur that many Christians have made moral progress and abhor the racism that fueled Nazi morality. But is this a "belief that has been common to nearly all Christians at all times" as the preface of Mere Christianity promises?[3] The answer is almost certainly no.

For most of Christian history, we Christians have been opposed to Judaism. We have demonstrated this theological dogma with repeated episodes of physical violence to Jews, Jewish holy books, synagogues, and Jewish property. We Christians have a tendency to forget such episodes, but the historical evidence cannot be denied. It is only recently that nearly all Christians have set Christian morality in opposition to violence against Jews. German Christian theologians like Walter Grundmann exploited this all-too-Christian tendency in their effort to remove all Jews and Jewish elements from Christianity.

It was called the Institute for the Study and Elimination of Jewish Influence on German Church Life. It was largely composed of Protestant (Lutheran) clergy and quickly found cross-denominational support.

> The Institute's goals were stated forthrightly at its opening by Grundmann, who delivered the keynote lecture on "The Dejudaization of the Religious Life as the Task of German Theology and Church." The present era, he declared, was similar to the Reformation: Protestants had to overcome Judaism just as Luther had overcome Catholicism. "The elimination of Jewish influence on German life is the urgent and fundamental question of the present German religious situation." Yes, Grundmann noted, people in Luther's day could not imagine Christianity without the Pope, just as today they could not imagine salvation without the Old Testament, but the goal could be realized. . . . The Bible would have to be purified, Grundmann continued, restored to its pristine condition, to proclaim the truth about Jesus: that he sought the destruction of Judaism.[4]

I desperately want to believe Lewis and affirm that Christian morality and Nazi morality stand in necessary opposition. From a "core Christian beliefs" standpoint, I can. (I teach my students this very thing: most of the Bible is written by Jews, for other Jews, on topics of Jewish theology. It is therefore impossible to "dejudaize" Christianity; if attempted, nothing would be left.) But from a Jewish-Christian borders perspective, the question becomes more complicated. Far too many people have taken to heart what Ignatius wrote to the second generation of Christians: "It is monstrous to confess Jesus Christ and to practice Judaizing."[5] Grundmann and his fellow German Christians did not view Christian morality in opposition to Nazi morality. Many attempted to marry Christianity to Nazism by divorcing it from Judaism. Tragically, they were able to find a longstanding Christian tradition to support their agenda.

In support of Lewis's division of Christian and Nazi moralities— and complicating matters further—it must be said that Nazi dogma was an evolving agenda. Eventually Nazism became decidedly anti-Christian. Heinrich Himmler (a key player in Nazi intelligentsia and policy) wrote, "We live in an era of the ultimate conflict with Christianity. It is part of the mission of the SS to give the German people in the next half century the non-Christian ideological foundations on which to lead and shape their lives."[6] Nazi clergy like Martin Niemoeller felt betrayed by Hitler's earlier promises to preserve a place for Christianity in the Third Reich.

It is true that Christian morality is not Nazi morality. But the opposite is also true. Lewis is much closer to the mark when he writes, "You will find this again and again about anything that is really Christian: every one is attracted by bits of it and wants to pick out those bits and leave the rest. . . . That is why people who are fighting for quite opposite things can both say they are fighting for Christianity."[7]

> It is true that Christian morality is not Nazi morality. But the opposite is also true.

If this were a book about Christian "best practices" or "what you need to know about Christian beliefs," we might live without the contradiction. But this is a book about borders and, especially, the borders shared by Jews and Christians. So we must ask,

How did Christian morality look in Nazi Europe? What dogmatic shape did it take? And if we find that it looked similar to the Christian moralities at work in the heresy hunting of early Christian theology, or Constantine's vision, or the Crusades, or our major church splits, or manifest destiny, or the Salem witch trials, or Confederate America, or the Red Scare, or countless acts of harm to LGBTQ+ children, should we not stop to wonder if there is a deeper sickness at work?

As already mentioned, there were Christians like Martin Niemoeller (a former Nazi) who fought the Nazi agenda to take control of Christian theology or church practice. Niemoeller started the Pastors Emergency League, which was the precursor to the Confessing Church movement. Niemoeller preached against Hitler's politics and was jailed for his efforts. He then spent seven years in concentration camps—Sachsenhausen and Dachau.

We Christians love heroic stories like this. I say this with a double tongue because I truly wish that more Christians were like Martin Niemoeller. I do not know if I would have his courage if faced with a similar situation. I hope that I would, but how can I say? Lewis reminds us that fortitude is one of the cardinal virtues. In leaving his Nazi status behind, Niemoeller became an exemplary man of fortitude. Very few are worthy of this word in the sense that Lewis intended.

I have also learned that there are no heroic stories related to the Holocaust. To tell this history with integrity, we must be true to the tragedy.

It is a false impression that "Niemoeller and his colleagues were standing up for Jews. On the contrary, they were standing up for Christians and for two very important bulwarks within the Christian tradition." Historian Robert Ericksen explains that the Confessing Church stood against the German Christian push to remove the Old Testament from the Bible. The Confessing Church stood for the traditional Christian belief that baptism transforms a person and trumps racial categories. "It is important to note that most Christians who stood up for 'Jews' during the Nazi era almost always stood up for Christians who happened to be of Jewish descent."[8] With this in mind, consider the words of Niemoeller himself on Christian complicity in the Holocaust: "Christianity in Germany bears a greater responsibility before God than the National Socialists, the SS and the Gestapo. We ought to have recognized the Lord Jesus in the brother who suffered and was persecuted despite him being a communist or a Jew. . . . Are not we Christians much more to blame, am I not much more guilty, than many who bathed their hands in blood?"[9]

Martin Niemoeller is an example of a Lutheran who eventually realized that Christian morality must stand against Nazism. In his postwar life, he realized that he could have and should have done more. In comparison to the thousands (millions?) of Christians who actively supported National Socialism, Niemoeller's public voice stands out as exceptional. But I doubt that Niemoeller himself ever saw it like this. He is best known for his statement of Christian moral action in the face of Nazism: "First they came for the Communists, but I was not a Communist so I did not speak out. Then they came for the Socialists *and* the Trade Unionists, but I was neither, so I did not speak out. Then they came for the Jews, but I was not a Jew so I did not speak out. And when they came for me, there was no one left to speak out for me."[10]

Normally mainline Protestants hear this as a call to moral action toward social justice of all kinds. I wholeheartedly concur. In addition to this interpretation, we should also hear Niemoeller's words as a lamentable failure of Christian morality. Niemoeller is voicing his own failure to be moral in any way that Jesus would have recognized. We can only celebrate the person he became once we fully acknowledge the Christian he was by default. Above all, we must avoid celebrating ourselves as we remember activists like Niemoeller. The Holocaust is not a backdrop for Christian heroism. It represents the very worst episode of many Christian failures along many Jewish-Christian borders.

Pastoral Nazism

Katharina von Kellenbach's book *The Mark of Cain* details many specific examples of Nazis who covered up their involvement in mass murder. Some of these perpetrators were fully indoctrinated within neo-pagan ideology. Some were Christians. What most had in common was a postwar silence about their crimes. Sometimes entire families were invested in the false biography of a beloved perpetrator. Von Kellenbach writes of her experience after learning of her uncle's war crimes. "My father told outright fabrications and bullied me into silence whenever I raised questions about the husband of his cousin, whom he still admired."[11] Her book has influenced me in a number of ways as it relates to cultural memory, Christian ethics, multigenerational guilt, and so on. Here I will recount only the stories of two men that feature within her research: Schmidt and Ermann.

Hans Hermann Schmidt was among the Nazi officers tried and found guilty of the mass murders at the Buchenwald death camp. Schmidt was the chief legal officer and deputy commander of the camp. He oversaw thousands of executions in that capacity. By his own admission, he was often the one giving "the order to fire." More than 56,000 people were murdered at Buchenwald. In the final months of its operation, approximately five thousand people were killed every month. Schmidt was quite forthright about the scope and nature of his actions. He felt no need to hide them because he considered his use of lethal force legitimate as sanctioned by law. He was convinced himself that his duties functioned within legitimate structures established by governmental authorities.[12] In addition, Schmidt blamed the conditions of mass starvation in the Buchenwald site on advancing enemy armies.

It is not clear how Christian Schmidt claimed to be between 1933 and 1945. He had been a member of the Lutheran Church. Indeed his hometown minister, Pastor Schloemann, insisted on his moral character in a 1947 petition. Clearly his family and pastor considered him to be a good Christian even after his terrible admission. Schmidt adopted Nazi dogma at some point and then officially rejoined the Lutheran Church in 1948. I will not guess at the following: was he ever really a Christian? Was he once a Christian but then fell away? Was he not a Christian during the war and then restored to the faith postwar? Was he a Christian his entire life and incorporated Nazism into his faith for a time? Not only am I not qualified to answer these questions; I will feel suspicious of any theologian who claims to have an answer.

Schmidt stood trial for war crimes, was convicted, sentenced, and executed. He was on death row for three years. While awaiting execution, Schmidt was attended by the prison chaplain, a Lutheran pastor named Karl Ermann. Ermann was the chaplain of an American-run prison in Landsberg from 1949 to 1951.

Karl Ermann's responsibilities as a chaplain included visiting cells, conversing with prisoners, facilitating worship services, and recruiting prisoners for the choir. He also conducted secret support for the prisoners. This violated prison policy. He and others smuggled letters, passed information to family members and lawyers for Nazi networks. Ermann supported a postwar Nazi effort to raise money and provide legal assistance for war criminals. As far as can be known, Karl Ermann never claimed to be anything other than a Christian.

Pastor Ermann helped Schmidt draft a final statement before his execution. Schmidt's last words remain consistent with his insistence of innocence despite his acknowledgment of overseeing state-sanctioned executions. But Schmidt's statement has also been Christianized, hinting of his heavenly vindication: "Before the face of God, before whom I will stand in the next moment, I affirm that I am innocent of the crimes with which I have been charged. I declare that I have done nothing else than what you, sirs, are doing right now: I have executed orders that had been legally given to me. . . . I die innocent."[13]

This is Pastor Ermann's account of Schmidt's final words as quoted in one of his sermons. Ermann's theology is such that he seems to fully endorse mass murder as long as it is endorsed by the state. He preached that Schmidt and his fellow Nazis demonstrated an "upright and obedient walk" in their final days. Schmidt, according to Ermann, denied the accusations of his guilt because these accusations "contradicted the truth." It must be kept in mind that Schmidt never denied his key part in the extermination of Jews. Rather, he fought against the notion that his actions should be considered crimes or immoral. Schmidt, with Ermann's support, argued for innocence since his actions had been carried out under the "compulsion of military necessities."[14] Thus Ermann believed that any attempt to hold Nazi officers accountable for mass murder "contradicted the truth." In Ermann's view, Schmidt—although Schmidt admitted to ordering thousands of deaths—was to be commended for standing by his denial of guilt.

When questioned by his superiors, Ermann wrote of Schmidt's faith, vouching for its authenticity. Pastor Ermann was convinced that Schmidt confessed of every sin that required forgiveness.

Herr Schmidt rejoined the Protestant Church in 1948 out of sincere conviction and remained faithful to this belief to his end. During those three years there was scarcely a worship service in which he did not participate. He was an attentive listener to the word of God. . . . He did not treat confession as a mere lip service but was cognizant of much guilt and omission in his life of which he spoke openly. But he could not come to an affirmation of the guilt ascribed to him by the court even though he examined his conscience thoroughly. . . . His guilt before God he confessed truthfully in both his last celebration of the Confession and of Holy Communion, and he received forgiveness of his sins with a desiring heart.[15]

Schmidt and Ermann are only two examples of Christians who married the dogma of Nazism with Christian dogma. One man oversaw and commanded the mass murder of thousands. The other man baptized this mass murder by refusing to interpret it as a sin. This monstrously evil narrative unfolds along the lines drawn by German Christian theologian Siegfried Leffler, who was quoted at the beginning of this chapter.

This too is a Jewish-Christian border. Sometimes the border is made of concrete and barbed wire. Sometimes the border is fortified by Christian theology.[16]

Dangerously Unexceptional

C. S. Lewis, as most people do, points to Nazism as an extreme form of evil. The people who followed the lead of Hitler and Schmidt were moral monsters. How can we argue with this in retrospect? Indeed the outcome of their sickness is impossible to miss. The danger in such thinking comes when Nazism is seen as exceptional, as something that could never happen again.

When Nazism is given a category all to itself, it might make it difficult to imagine genocide ever taking place in a civilized society. Of course, this is false. Hitler may well have been a calculating psychopath. Maybe an inordinate number of Nazis were. But what we cannot say is that every Nazi was exceptional. What if, as Hannah Arendt observed, many of these war criminals were just ordinary people who trusted the moral judgment of their leaders?[17] Wouldn't it be even more terrible to learn that evil, even the worst sorts, emerges from unexceptional places, from people who would strike us as boring and uninspired? In one of his very finest moments of genius, Lewis explains, "Of all the passions the passion for the Inner Ring is most skillful in making a man who is not yet a very bad man do very bad things." How does this happen? Lewis paints this picture:

> Obviously bad men, obviously threatening or bribing, will almost certainly not appear. Over a drink or a cup of coffee, disguised as a triviality and sandwiched between two jokes, from the lips of a man, or woman, whom you have recently been getting to know rather better and whom you hope to know better still—just at the moment when you are most anxious not to appear crude, or naive or a prig—the hint will come. It will be the hint of something, which is not quite in accordance with the technical rules of fair play, something that the public, the ignorant, romantic public, would never understand. Something which even the outsiders in your own profession are apt to make a fuss about, but something, says your new friend, which "we"—and at the word "we" you try

not to blush for mere pleasure—something "we always do." And you will be drawn in, if you are drawn in, not by desire for gain or ease, but simply because at that moment, when the cup was so near your lips, you cannot bear to be thrust back again into the cold outer world. It would be so terrible to see the other man's face—that genial, confidential, delightfully sophisticated face—turn suddenly cold and contemptuous, to know that you had been tried for the Inner Ring and rejected. And then, if you are drawn in, next week it will be something a little further from the rules, and next year something further still, but all in the jolliest, friendliest spirit. It may end in a crash, a scandal, and penal servitude: it may end in millions, a peerage and giving the prizes at your old school. But you will be a scoundrel.[18]

This is a scenario that sounds more like office politics than the hell of war. War, especially if we imagine it from within a totalitarian state, eventually dispenses with subtlety. I am more worried about the roots of the problem, and I believe that Lewis aptly describes the subtle gestures that give evil a foothold. Or consider racism. The passing on of racism is even more subtle than office politics. Instead of a slow descent from upstanding citizen to scoundrel, most racism is a lifelong and multigenerational indoctrination. Worse still, no one is immune.

I think that the just-following-orders explanation will never explain evils like Nazism unless there is some amoral default setting (like racism or anti-Judaism) at work as well. In the case of anti-Judaism, it festered within Christian dogma for centuries. Christianity (historically speaking) is so inclined to anti-Judaism that Christians can easily slip into hostility toward Jews without much self-awareness. Lewis's analogy of office politics should serve as a warning:

I live in the Managerial Age, in a world of "Admin." The greatest evil is not now done in those sordid "dens of crime" that Dickens loved to paint. It is not done even in concentration camps and labour camps. In those we see its final result. But it is conceived and ordered (moved, seconded, carried, and minuted) in clean, carpeted, warmed and well-lighted offices, by quiet men with white collars and cut fingernails and smooth-shaven cheeks who do not need to raise their voices. Hence, naturally enough, my symbol for Hell is something like the bureaucracy of a police state or the office of a thoroughly nasty business concern.[19]

The friends and family of Hans Hermann Schmidt thoroughly endorsed him. Schmidt, who oversaw the daily mass murders at Buchenwald was "perceived as a nice and respectable man in his private life not only in the eyes of the prison chaplain, but also in his hometown and by his family."[20]

If Lewis is right, if the worst sorts of evil emerge from the veneer of civil institutions and quiet men, something as terrible as mass murder does not require a singular cult of personality. It is far too convenient to blame a single, psychopathic dictator or oligarchy. An evil like genocide is too often an institutional sin supported by generations of subtle gestures, jokes, quietly held beliefs, and averted eyes. If so it is crucial that we Christians become more self-aware than we have been. Even our subtle gestures toward anti-Judaism can undo the moral progress we have made with Jewish-Christian relations. You don't need to look far before discovering vocabulary that betrays our longer legacy of anti-Jewish dogma.

Underdogma

As I have repeated several times in this book—and do it here again for emphasis—my experience of Christians and evangelicals especially suggests that anti-Semitism is fading.

The accusation of Jews for murdering Christ is also less prominent. Some denominations have attempted to correct this accusation with public retractions of historic dogma. But our historic leanings toward anti-Judaism are still quite prevalent. Children's programs and Sunday-school material are perhaps the most disheartening. Christian authors, artists, youth pastors, and parents continue unwittingly to promote a negative view of Pharisees and other Jewish characters in the New Testament. It is then no wonder that when Christian children grow up, they continue to betray Christianity's anti-Jewish legacy in the vocabulary they use. Even with all of the progress we've made, it is still quite common for Christians to call out other Christians as modern legalists or hypocrites, just like "the Jews" in Jesus' day—or for short, Pharisees.

In both my evangelical upbringing and in my present mainline Protestant setting, I continue to witness unconscious anti-Judaism. As a seminary professor I can see that this tendency spans denominations, racial divides, and political orientations. But—and I lament this—anti-Jewish vocabulary is especially egregious on the lips of my fellow mainliners. Even those of us who pursue social justice and despise prejudice continue to betray the dogmatic legacy of anti-Judaism. I notice the tendency to accuse fellow Christians of Pharisaism most often in political disputes.

From experience, I can say that few of us know that we are saying anything anti-Jewish. When I point this out to my blue-state coreligionists, the correction tends to be almost immediate and comes with a sense of shame. Most often the anti-Jewish logic goes unchecked. Allow me to spell out the pattern. First, we mainliners pick a particular underdog (to use Cornel West's word) to defend. Second, we identify a systematic power that oppresses our underdog. Third, we endeavor to lend religious legitimacy to our position by recalling Jesus' support for underdogs in the first century. Fourth—and this is where the anti-Judaism enters—we create a narrative that equates modern oppressors with Jesus' enemies. We call the oppressors Pharisees. In this pattern, Jesus' modern enemies are often Christian leaders who cling to tradition to the detriment of the underdogs.

New Testament scholar Amy-Jill Levine has an interesting take on this pattern. Levine, as a vocal advocate for Jewish well-being, wishes that progressive Christians had a higher Christology. Why would a (self-described) Yankee Jewish feminist want such a thing? It's simple: when progressive Christians are not quite convinced of Jesus' divinity, they attempt to elevate him in other ways. If mainline Protestants suffer from a low Christology, they will make an effort to degrade Jesus' contemporaries so as to elevate Jesus. In this process of elevating Jesus by degrading his fellow Jews, Jesus becomes a social reformer. But if we had a sufficiently high Christology—if Jesus already occupies the place of divinity—we would not need to demote anyone in order to exalt Jesus. Levine writes that for low-Christology Christians, "Jesus has to be unique, and good; therefore his Jewish context has to represent everything that 'good' people resist."[21] Levine sees this tendency, for example, in the theological musings of President Jimmy Carter.

> If mainline Protestants suffer from a low Christology, they will make an effort to degrade Jesus' contemporaries so as to elevate Jesus. In this process of elevating Jesus by way of degrading his fellow Jews, Jesus becomes a social reformer.

I admire the life of Jimmy Carter. In many ways, Carter's life is the example of a socially active evangelical with a moral compass. Part of what I love about Carter is what Rabbi Shmuley Boteach calls "Mr. Carter's underdog obsession," or simply his "underdogma."[22] This label was not meant affectionately. Even so, I find it an endearing quality of the former president. It therefore pains me to say that Carter is among the worst culprits of progressive, American anti-Judaism. I do not believe that Carter himself knows the potential harm of his words. I will not provide his most anti-Jewish statements. Rather, these paragraphs typify his common, well-intentioned remarks. In a book meant for Christian devotional study, Carter writes:

> During almost ten decades in the South—and throughout America—very few of us, even in our churches, condemned or criticized total racial segregation. We accepted the legal premise of "separate but equal." . . . Even the most enlightened pastors would say, "Well, that's a social problem. We just preach the gospel." We shake our heads now, but that's the way we lived back then, and that was the way we had lived for generations. We accepted the "fact" that we white folks were "superior" and that people of a different color were "inferior."
>
> In the time of Christ, the Jews believed that Gentiles stood outside the purview of God's covenant with Abraham. Naturally, this caused Jews to feel superior. But in this encounter with the people of Nazareth, his hometown, Jesus emphasized that God wants to bless all of us, simply because God loves us. . . . Jesus says, "Love others, regardless of who they are." Let's pray that we might eliminate discrimination, animosity, and grudges from our lives as followers of Jesus Christ.[23]

I hope that my readers agree that Carter's intentions are admirable. This is a call for social justice in the face of racism. I appreciate that Carter believes that there is no room for racism within moral Christianity. But here—subtly—is where his anti-Judaism enters. In Carter's logic, when Americans are at our worst, when we are most racist, we are just like the Jews or, worse, the Pharisees. Here are a few other examples from Carter:

> Jews despised publicans. . . . I think that Jesus wants each of us to ask, "Am I more like the Pharisee or the publican?" And then, "How might I need to change?"[24]

> The Jews of Jesus' day despised men like Matthew.[25]

> Are we careful that only our friends or people similar to us come into our presence? It's a natural human trait. We want to protect ourselves. We don't want unsavory people of unpredictable behavior to encroach upon our personal privileges or priorities.
>
> How very different was the life of Jesus Christ, our Savior! He was condemned and questioned by his own people because he reached out to tax-collectors, hated by the Jews and used by the Romans.[26]

> Love and forgiveness are not easy. First-century Jews thought it generous to forgive someone three times; Peter upped the ante and suggested seven times. Jesus replied, "Multiply that number by seventy." . . . God calls us to develop an unlimited capacity to forgive.[27]

Carter's version of Jesus' gospel is a mantra of love for the socially disempowered. I believe that this is an important, indeed crucial, message. But time and again Carter emphasizes Jesus' love at the expense of "the Jews." Notice the lack of qualification: he does not say "many Jews despised" or "some Jews hated"; Carter reinforces the age-old stereotype by painting all Jews in Jesus' time as hateful, elitist, and worse. Surely Carter knows that Jesus, Peter, and almost all of the characters in the Gospels are Jewish. What is unclear is whether Carter knows that Jesus and the Pharisees had a great deal in common. Far from being the hateful elitists or hypocrites of Christian imagination, the historical Pharisees were among the most liberal readers of legal instruction and the most representative of common folk in Jesus' day.

This association with traditionalist Christians and first-century Jews/Pharisees has surfaced often in the American debate over LGBTQ+ rights. After Carter made multiple statements in support of gay marriage, many conservative Christians criticized him for it. These critics often cited biblical passages in defense of "traditional family values." After one online article, a commenter defending Carter wrote, "Pharisees need to quit proof-texting to blame their bigotries on God." Another comment in the same vein said, "Unlike many who post here, Mr. Carter is a Christian—not a proof-texting Pharisee—and understands that Jesus said 'Love God,' 'Love your neighbor,' and 'Judge not.'" Clearly this comment borrows from a very ancient Jewish-Christian border (the Christian caricature of love versus legalism) and has repurposed it for a divide between liberal and conservative Christianity. Helpfully, another commenter wrote in reply, "You have a potential anti-Semitism issue regarding Pharisees. Most Pharisees were dedicated teachers of the Torah. Jesus condemned some of them, but in an ironic way. He said they sat in the seat of Moses . . . a positive . . . and Paul called himself a Pharisee."[28]

What this commenter does—what Carter and his defenders fail to do—is to hint at a nuanced description of first-century Jewish culture. In their first-century context, Pharisees varied widely in a number of respects. But even when their general characteristics are summarized, they do not turn out to be all that different from Jesus. Jesus probably argues most often with the Pharisees because he has the most in common with them.[29] But in the binary world of red states and blue states, we often need Jesus to be the singular crusader for social justice in a way that contrasts him with Jewish legalism. Not only is this bad history; it undermines the "underdogma" of liberal Christianity by reinforcing an even older injustice: anti-Judaism.

I am not accusing Carter or LGBTQ+ activists of anti-Semitism. Anti-Semitism is a form of racism that often develops alongside anti-Judaism. I will deal with the ideology of anti-Judaism more fully in the next chapter. At present, let's just note that one does not need to be a moral monster to parrot the Christian pattern of anti-Judaism. The life and legacy of Jimmy Carter is altogether dissimilar from the Nazis mentioned above. The reason that Carter works as an example on this topic is that few people will doubt his good intentions. Even those who disparage his politics do not often attack his character. I could have just as easily pointed to

> I am not accusing Carter or LGBTQ+ activists of anti-Semitism. Anti-Semitism is a form of racism that often develops alongside anti-Judaism. . . . At present, let's just note that one does not need to be a moral monster to parrot the Christian pattern of anti-Judaism.

Pope Francis, another well-intentioned activist for the underdog. Francis, whom I admire a great deal, teaches that the Pharisees were "rigid on the outside, but, as Jesus said of them, 'rotting in the heart,' weak, weak to the point of rottenness."[30]

What makes Francis's statement all the more depressing is that he as a theologian should know better. He ought to know that many modern Jews trace their heritage to the Pharisees. This statement—especially because the intention is to promote love—has wounded some of my Jewish friends who are otherwise inspired by Pope Francis. C. S. Lewis falls into the same trap in his call for Christians to avoid hatred. In Lewis's *Reflections on the Psalms*, he condemns the author of Psalm 139:

> Almost comically the Psalmist of 139 asks "Don't I hate those who hate thee, Lord? . . . Why, I hate them as if they were *my* enemies" (21, 22). Now obviously all this—taking upon oneself to hate those whom one thinks God's enemies, avoiding the society of those one thinks wicked, judging our neighbours, thinking oneself "too good" for some of them . . . is an extremely dangerous, almost fatal game. It leads straight to "Pharisaism" in the sense which Our Lord's own teaching has given to that word. . . .[31]

Lewis then writes that an "evil" is at work within this psalm: the evil of Pharisaism. As I pause to consider Lewis's words, my underdogma moves me in two directions simultaneously. I tend to agree with Lewis that "taking upon oneself to hate those whom one thinks God's enemies" is extremely dangerous. I am not at all comfortable with this passage of Scripture. But I wonder if the psalmist's feelings are more understandable if we grant that this psalm was written from a place of extreme oppression or exile. If so, is not Lewis too quick to condemn this passage as evil? Perhaps the passage needs to be nuanced by historical context. It is only within such nuance that such an indictment can be heard with integrity.

What can certainly not be excused is the straight line Lewis draws from hatred and evil to "Pharisaism." Three points must be considered: (1) Pharisaism is not a word used in the Bible; rather, it derives from centuries of Christians slandering the forerunners to the rabbis; (2) while some Pharisees are slandered in the New Testament, hatred is not part of the accusation; (3) we mainline Protestants are (I hope) diametrically opposed to the results of anti-Judaism, so should we not avoid using its vocabulary?

Words Shape Worlds

In the previous chapter, I pointed to the horrifically influential words of Martin Luther. I suggested that his advice to German officials influenced the anti-Jewish (and eventually anti-Semitic) world of National Socialism. The extent of Luther's theological impact on German Christians and Nazi dogma is open to debate. What cannot be denied is the fact that centuries of dehumanization of Jews and demonization of Judaism created the context whereby some Christian theologians supported and defended the Holocaust. Luther's words certainly exist along this trajectory. We must ask, Do our words exist along this trajectory? Is our vocabulary informed by this legacy? Does it contribute to this legacy? I would challenge my readers to keep these questions in mind the next time they watch a church play designed for children. What sort of nuance is being taught about first-century Jews from the pulpit or at Sunday school?

This chapter included the stories of two Christian Nazis: Ermann and Schmidt. I imagine that most of my readers will find their notion of Christian morality and dogma to be repulsive. What is crucial to recognize is that this ideology didn't evolve overnight. Theologically motivated anti-Judaism is much, much older than Luther's venom. It might take years before a pattern of thought can become public policy. But consider this: we Christians have a two-thousand-year legacy of dehumanizing the Pharisees and the Jews more generally. Christian complicity in the Holocaust is not a hypothetical problem. It is modern history. We know that Christian anti-Judaism can and does result in violence against Jews. However we shape Christian morality, it must begin with the words we choose, the stories we tell, and lessons learned from our history of mistakes.

CHAPTER 5

On the Border of Anti-Judaism and Philo-Judaism

They say that after eating the mountain-apple and the earthquake, when things in our country had all gone awry, the Landlord's Son himself became one of his Father's tenants and lived among us, for no other purpose than that he should be killed. The Stewards themselves do not know clearly the meaning of their story: hence, if you ask them how the slaying of the Son should help us, they are driven to monstrous answers.

—MR. WISDOM FROM C. S. LEWIS'S *THE PILGRIM'S REGRESS*

It has been said that English literature has portrayed the Jew as the best of saints and the worst of sinners but never as the simple human being. This characterizes more than English literature; it characterizes the Christian view of Israel.

—RICHARD L. RUBENSTEIN

Ed's Library

Ed was my wife's grandfather and an important person to many. He was especially important to me. His parishioners had called him Charles or Chuck. After his career as a Presbyterian pastor was over, his psychiatric clients called him Dr. Peacock. Owing to his uncanny Donald Duck impression, my kids called him Papa Duck. When I knew him he went by his first syllable—Ed.

Edward Charles Peacock was struck by polio at the age of twelve. He lived for a time within an iron lung. He was confined to a wheelchair in a world not ready to understand or accommodate disability. His entire adulthood was spent navigating the increasingly painful brokenness of post-polio syndrome. At the age of seventy-seven, his post-polio had become unbearable. On Monday, June 18, 2012, Ed told his wife that he would die on Friday. The hospice nurse scolded him, telling him that he might live for another two years or more. I hugged his neck and told him that he had another rebound in him. But he had stopped eating. He died—just like he promised—on Friday, June 22, 2012. I was given the tasks of preaching at his funeral and sorting out his library.

Ed's library was a tangle of his investments in psychology, theology, classics, philosophy, and American history. It was a small room and the shelves had outgrown it. His books winded their way down the hallway and into his bedroom like untended vines. The library was an extension of him. Even after he could no longer push his wheelchair down the hallway himself, he took joy in telling me where to find one of his books. I met the work of Martin Buber in Ed's library. I met the Jewish voices of Baruch Spinoza and Abraham Geiger in Ed's library. I also encountered a book titled *A World without Jews*, a collection of writings by Karl Marx in the same library. For better and worse, it was a transport into bygone generations of intelligentsia. Sorting through his books brought back the many and varied conversations we had shared.

When I left town for seminary, he gave me his *Theological Dictionary of the New Testament* (ten volumes). Ed loved this bright teal shelf of books like other men love red Corvettes. He actually giggled with glee as he told me, "This series is one of *the* major achievements of modern New Testament scholarship." Most of my fellow seminarians called this set *TDNT*. Ed called these books after the name of their chief editor, "Kittel."

For years after he would ask me about Kittel. "Are you finding

Kittel useful?" Ed would remind me of the immense value of
Kittel for students of New Testament Greek. It was as if 1930s
German theologian Gerhard Kittel was a dear friend who had
moved abroad. It wasn't just because Kittel was among the gems of
his library; it was about our connection, he and I. Our love of language was something we shared in common. Of course he loved
the books, but he was really expressing his love for me.

I had indeed used the volumes often and had taken to calling them Kittel just like Ed did. Their chief value, I found, was
in etymology. This set of volumes provides a dictionary, but it
also provides the study of words in ancient literary contexts. The
careful reader can thus follow a word's evolution. Admittedly, it is
almost too much information; Kittel is decadent in a super nerdy
sort of way.

I think that I had owned Kittel for five years before I learned
about the Nazi affiliations of many of the *TDNT* contributors.
Some of the Christian scholars who contributed to *TDNT* were
openly anti-Semitic. Others harbored a more deeply rooted anti-
Judaism. (Anti-Judaism is a very old Christian stance against a
particular view of Jewish religion. It is a theological position that is
still present in today's church and can foster anti-Semitism when
married to racial prejudice.) Gerhard Kittel's writings betrayed
both his anti-Judaism and his anti-Semitism.

This revelation shocked me, probably more that it should
have. Kittel was a German intellectual living in the 1930s, after
all! The name Kittel had always brought to mind Ed's smiling
eyes and glowing endorsements. So I was scandalized when I
encountered Gerhard Kittel's short essay "The Jewish Question."
Thereafter I couldn't help but associate the name Kittel with his
exhortations in this essay to revoke citizenship from German Jews
and to forbid them sexual relations with non-Jews. This discovery

about Kittel was also perplexing to me because Ed was committed to philo-Semitism (friendship to Jews and Judaism). I remember him calling Jewish rabbis "my brothers" in his nerdy but genuine voice. How could the least anti-Semitic person I knew endorse Gerhard Kittel?

Ed shook his head in what I took to be resignation. He explained that the world was a different place in those days. It was one of the few times that Ed didn't beam with joy when we were discussing scholarship. Then he told me where to find his Martin Buber collection. Ed was a man of peace. Perhaps he thought that Buber's voice of peace would be a way to feed my interests. He was not entirely wrong. Buber's life was something of a bridge in a time when most were building walls. As much as I admire Martin Buber, my interests were not about getting along and finding common ground. I wanted a way into the problem and better tools for navigating it.

As I was researching for this chapter I learned that Gerhard Kittel's active support of the Nazi Party was even more egregious than I previously knew. He was a key player in Nazi intelligentsia. Not only did his anti-Semitism color his academic work, he authored several articles of Nazi propaganda. Not only was Kittel among the more influential Christians in Germany, he was among the most vocal Nazi ideologues. I do not believe that Ed knew much of this.

Not only was Kittel among the more influential Christians in Germany, he was among the most vocal Nazi ideologues.

I don't really need Kittel anymore. I now have language software and online tools that are far more helpful. I could probably use the shelf space for something else. I keep the books for Ed's sake. My library, now tangled with Ed's books, includes several bizarre relics from previous generations. The shelf that boasts the teal, ten-volume *Theological Dictionary of the New Testament* sends my memory in two directions at once: toward Kittel's anti-Semitism and toward Ed's philo-Semitism.

The Risk of Philo-Semitism

In their exploration of race and religion in America, Michael Emerson and Christian Smith observe that many American evangelicals are well-intentioned. The authors "move beyond the old idea that racial problems result from ignorant, prejudiced, mean people (and that evangelicals are such people). This is simply inaccurate." Rather, Emerson and Smith "explore the ways in which culture, values, norms, and organizational features that are quintessentially evangelical and quintessentially American, despite having many positive qualities, paradoxically have negative effects on race relations."[1] There is, I think, a similar lesson to be learned about the ways that Christians think about Jews and Judaism. As I pointed out in the previous chapter, we can and do participate in problematic patterns of thought. This does not mean, however, that our intentions are necessarily impure. I have found that many Christians intend to be friendly to Jews (what is sometimes called philo-Semitism) but contribute to anti-Jewish patterns of thought without knowing it. I have also found that many Christians contributing to these patterns of thought are otherwise intelligent and well-educated.

Remarkably, many forms of anti-Judaism and anti-Semitism stem not from ignorance and mean-spirited inclinations but from intense focus by intellectual elites. The ivory tower has a long history of interest in theological, economic, social, and racial theories about Jews and Judaism. It often takes generations for these patterns of thought to become the common sense of regular folk. David Nirenberg begins his wide-ranging book *Anti-Judaism:*

The Western Tradition, with this line: "For several thousand years people have been thinking about Judaism." Nirenberg sets out his project by asking, "Why did so many diverse cultures—even many with no Jews living among them—think so much about Judaism? What work did thinking about Judaism do for them in their efforts to make sense of their world? . . . And how did this history of thinking about Judaism affect the future possibilities of existence for living Jews?"[2]

Nirenberg surveys the ideas that generated social realities in Egypt, early and medieval Christianities, Islam, the Spanish Inquisition, the Reformation, Shakespeare's England, and so on. He shows that time after time some of the most influential ideas have used Jews or Judaism as a point of departure. In this process, great minds have often committed the sin of inventing fantasies of what they imagine Judaism to be. The next step in this process is almost always an attempt to triumph over the fantasy, to show how a better society can be created if only the pitfalls of Judaism are overcome. I call this the "mythological foothold."

Christians are not the only folk to focus on the idea of Judaism. We have, perhaps, been doing it the longest. The apostle Paul advised Christians to "pray without ceasing." We never quite managed to figure this out. Instead, we have come very close to *thinking about Jews and Judaism* without ceasing for two thousand years.

If you walk into one hundred different synagogues on one hundred different Saturdays, you might never hear a single mention of Christians or Christianity. By contrast, most Christian worship services—and there are many, many more of these—regularly refer to Jews and Judaism. Of course we do. Almost all of the Christian Bible was composed by Jews. Most of early Christian theology was either adapted from Judaism or composed in departure from Judaism. We believe that our God established a special relationship with Israel. Our Messiah is Jewish. For better or worse, Christians simply cannot stop thinking about "the Jews."

Would it surprise you to learn that many Jews find great discomfort in this? Would it surprise you to hear that many Jews (I will not say most because I do not rightly know) would prefer to have Christians focus on something else? Can we blame our Jewish friends for wishing that we would talk about someone, something, *anything* else? Take a moment to consider this. How would we Christians feel if a neighboring group that outnumbered us by billions could not stop discussing us, in most cases without our presence or permission? Now imagine that this same group has a long history of trying to convert us, punctuated by determined efforts to murder us? Wouldn't we want those billions of people to just leave us alone? Even if billions of these folks said kind things about us and even if most of them meant well, wouldn't we want them to focus elsewhere?

> How would we Christians feel if a neighboring group that outnumbered us by billions could not stop discussing us, and in most cases without our presence or permission?

The book before you, of course, borders a similar problem. I am convinced that as long as Christians have Bibles, we will never stop thinking about Jews and Judaism. So we may as well try to do it better than we have. In order to do this, we must learn to recognize and reflect on the ways that we have created worldviews by generating "'pathological' fantasies of Judaism."[3] I am also convinced that seeking mutual understanding in dialogue is necessary. But even with this conviction, I acknowledge that I have and will make missteps and possibly contribute to the very problem that I am attempting to address. Friendship (as I will discuss more in my chapter on love) comes with risks. I continue to believe that Jewish-Christian friendship is worth the risk. Even so, we must be aware of these risks.

One of the chief dangers of learning about a group of people (ancient or modern) is overgeneralization. Overgeneralizations and stalk narratives—be they positive or negative—can dehumanize. Philosopher Ted Cohen addresses the problem of creating narratives about groups of people that generalize their traits. Cohen explains that "stereotypes can be annoying, just as such, without regard to whether they are negative." He continues: "In 'Concerning the Jews,' Mark Twain offers an exceedingly flattering characterization of the Jews, and it troubles me almost as much as the negative portraits offered by T. S. Eliot and Edith Wharton. A stereotype can rob you of your particularity just as surely if it is flattering as if it is negative."[4]

Consider the stereotype of intelligence and bookishness that follows Jewish identity. I bring this up because a similar devotion to bookishness unites me with several of my Jewish friends. Cornel West writes of this affinity, "In my own life, my interaction with Jewish intellectuals—not that I thought of them as such then—was critical in terms of my growth and development."[5] This interaction was critical, in part, because West's upbringing tended toward "a certain anti-intellectualism" whereby ideas were important if they only had "instrumental value."[6]

From a Christian perspective, Jewish culture does not suffer from the same tendency. West expresses his admiration for Jewish culture wherein ideas have a life of their own. Seemingly, by comparison, many Jewish families promote the life of the mind. Michael Lerner (in dialogue with West) explains the reason for this perception by tracing the impetus for Jewish education back to the ancient world: "So where does a Jewish man become a man, if he can't compete on the same grounds as the dominant culture? The answer is, he does it by becoming a scholar, a reader of texts, or a scribe, someone who can act out his prowess in the realm of written words. . . . After about two thousand years of practicing this kind of mind development . . . the intellectual skills developed enabled Jews to be successful in the intellectual, cultural, and economic pursuits that are rewarded in the modern capitalist world."[7]

I identify strongly with Cornel West's observation of cultural anti-intellectualism within segments of Christianity. In my experience, there is a strong fundamentalist drive to resist intellectual complication in the church, especially when it comes to faith. I greatly admire my Jewish friends who desire complexity in their Bible study and theological reflection. I also, like West, owe a great debt to many Jewish mentors in my life who have invested in my intellectual development.

Lerner's summary of Jewish cultural history, therefore, sheds light on an important Jewish-Christian difference, and one that is important to me especially. Praise of Jewish culture—be it intellectual investment, humor, or history—can lead to a posture of philo-Semitism among Christians. But allow me to use this exchange between West and Lerner to point out a common misstep in Jewish-Christian dialogue.

What West perceives and Lerner confirms is an overgeneralized explanation of a cultural difference. What neither does is contest the stereotype. Perhaps it goes without saying that some Christians are indeed as intellectual as Cornel West. And perhaps it goes without saying that not every Jew is well-educated or seeks to monetize his or her cultural legacy. But by not nuancing these statements some readers will simply take away or reinforce stereotypes.

What makes Lerner's summary even more problematic is that it comes from an intelligent and well-educated rabbi. When told to a Christian conversation partner, there is an implicit invitation to believe and repeat the stereotype.[8]

Some stereotypes are built upon generalizations that are mostly or partly true. And, as West illustrates, it is seemingly innocent to build up a religious neighbor with positive statements that are mostly true. But the danger of the stereotype is still there. Stereotypes that create friendship among some will reinforce fear or misgiving in others. In Lerner's summary, the explanation is that Jews value higher learning, are money motivated, or are intellectually competitive. Some folks who believe this may say, "I like Jews because they are smart and good business people."[9] Others may perceive the very same stereotypes and become resentful or

> Stereotypes that create friendship among some will reinforce fear or misgiving in others.

suspicious. Before moving forward, I will reiterate my point for clarity: even when the stereotype is mostly true, or mostly positive, it can have harmful and lasting results.

Rabbi Richard Rubenstein observes that Christians are almost incapable of seeing Jews without also imagining a theological narrative. Many Christians view Israel as a nation with special divine revelation and relationship. I will explore Rubenstein's argument more fully below. The gist is that Jews seem to be a part of an indispensible Christian theology. Gary Porton suggests that if Rubenstein is correct, "Christianity cannot imagine the Jew as a normal human being."[10]

Just as it is possible to dehumanize our friends by negativity, it is possible to dehumanize our friends by elevating them. It might seem, then, that the line between philo-Semitism and anti-Semitism is paper-thin. The relationship between them is real and precarious. I will argue below that I do not think that philo-Semitism *necessarily* collapses into theological fantasy. But before we move too quickly to a solution, we must acknowledge the high stakes of dehumanizing Jews for the purpose of a theological narrative.

David Nirenberg explains how "across several thousand years, myriad lands, and many different spheres of activity, people have used ideas about Jews and Judaism to fashion the tools with which they construct the reality of their world."[11] Certainly, as I already mentioned, this is true of Christian theology. Consider these words of Martin Luther, which are seemingly generous in spirit: "We are but Gentiles, while the Jews are of the lineage of Christ. We are aliens and in-laws; they are blood relatives, cousins, and brothers of our Lord. Therefore, if one is to boast of flesh and blood, the Jews are actually nearer to Christ than we are."[12]

C. S. Lewis says something almost identical in a quotation discussed earlier in this book. Lewis wrote that "we christened gentiles, are after all the graft, the wild vine, possessing 'joys not promised to our birth'; though perhaps we do not think of this so often as we might."[13] Or consider Lewis's indictment of Hitler's anti-Semitism:

> I might agree that the Allies are partly to blame, but nothing can fully excuse the iniquity of Hitler's persecution of the Jews, or the absurdity of his theoretical position. Did you see that he said "The Jews have made no contribution to human culture and in crushing them I am doing the will of the Lord"? Now as the whole idea of the "Will of the Lord" is precisely what the world owes to the Jews, the blaspheming tyrant has just fixed his absurdity for all to see in a single sentence, and shown that he is as contemptible for his stupidity as he is detestable for his cruelty. For the German people as a whole we ought to have charity; but for dictators, "Nordic" tyrants and so on—well, read the chapter about Mr. Savage in [The Pilgrim's Regress] and you have my views.[14]

Here we see in Lewis the natural tendency to call out anti-Semitism for its irrationality. I am not so certain that "the Jews" in general are to be credited for the idea of God's will. Certainly many ancient Jews gave momentum to this idea. No doubt, Lewis's elevation of the Jews in overgeneralized terms stands in reaction to Hitler. One does not engage the ideas of Adolf Hitler without dirtying oneself. My point here is that even in philo-Semitism, we Christians are inclined to misrepresent "the Jews." I do not doubt that I have been guilty of this too from time to time.

In both of the sources mentioned here—Luther and Lewis—we can find other statements about "the Jews" that are deeply disturbing. Generalizing in positive terms can easily turn to equally generalized venom. This is not to say that it always does, but the risk is there along with countless precedents. And if we imagine Judaism as a positive theological exemplar, the consequence is that Judaism can easily become a negative theological foil—or as I have put it, a mythological foothold.

I hope that the whole of this book indicates that I believe philo-Semitism to be necessary and that it can enhance one's faith as a Christian. I am well-aware that what I have written in this chapter might seem discouraging to well-intentioned Christians. I promise not to conclude with a Marsh-wiggled attitude of Jewish-Christian friendship. Alas, the problem gets worse before it gets better.

The Mythological Foothold

John Chrysostom (c. 349–407) was known for his powerful and influential preaching. *Chrysostom* means "golden mouthed." Christian historians remember Chrysostom in mostly positive terms. Cardinal John Henry Newman once wrote that he was a "bright, cheerful, gentle soul; a sensitive heart, a temperament open to emotion and impulse; and all this elevated, refined, transformed by the touch of heaven . . . winning followers, riveting affections, by his sweetness, frankness, and neglect of self."[15]

Chrysostom is also remembered for speaking out against false doctrine, abuse of doctrine, and abuse of authority. So the power of his preaching sometimes became a targeted effort against a religious enemy. Chrysostom was convinced that the Christian was beset on all sides by heresy. Jews, in his view, were not just part of the problem of heretical borders; they typified the problem. Christians inclined to celebrate at Jewish festivals were thus in spiritual danger. He spoke of Jews in zoological terms: "such beasts are not fit for work, they are fit for killing." Here is a fuller context:

> Jewish people were driven by their drunkenness and plumpness to the ultimate evil; they kicked about, they failed to accept the yoke of Christ, nor did they pull the plow of his teaching. Another prophet hinted at this when he said: "Israel is as obstinate as a stubborn heifer." And still another called the Jews "an untamed calf." Although such beasts are unfit for work, they are fit for killing. And this is what happened to the Jews: while they were making themselves unfit for work, they grew fit for slaughter. This is why Christ said: "But as for these my enemies, who did not want me to be king over them, bring them here and slay them." You Jews should have fasted then, when drunkenness was doing those terrible things to you, when your gluttony was giving birth to your ungodliness—not now. Now your fasting is untimely and an abomination. Who said so? Isaiah himself when he called out in a loud voice: "I did not choose this fast, say the Lord." Why? "You quarrel and squabble when you fast and strike those subject to you with your fists." But if your fasting was an abomination when you were striking your fellow slaves, does it become acceptable now that you have slain your Master?[16]

Chrysostom's series of sermons against the Jews remains among the worst demonstrations of hate speech in history. Notice that in order to make his argument, Chrysostom assumes the authority of Scripture (both testaments) that was passed down in Jewish tradition. The fact that the Divine Voice can be heard through Jewish testimony, he suggests, makes the Jewish rejection of Christ most miserable. He assumes the special relationship between God and Israel and uses this elevated status to dehumanize them.

Chrysostom also repeats the false accusation that Jews—not Romans—killed Christ. "Nothing is more miserable than those people who never failed to attack their own salvation" (1.2.3). He holds Jewish education in high regard but this only makes them more culpable as "Slayers of Christ." He argues, "From their childhood they read the prophets, but they crucified him whom the prophets had foretold" (1.2.1). No other accusation has caused more dehumanization and violence to the Jewish people. In Chrysostom's view, they are now dogs: "Although those Jews had been called to the adoption of sons, they fell to kinship with dogs; we who were dogs received the strength, through God's grace, to put aside the irrational nature which was ours and to rise to the honor of sons. . . . Do you see how those who at first were children became dogs? Do you wish to find out how we, who at first were dogs, became children?" (1.2.1–2).

Here Chrysostom uses the all too common Christian pattern of elevating Jews for the purpose of creating a foothold. Once the Jewish status as divine children or prophetic forebears has been established, Christians can claim to be true heirs of this legacy.

I will say one more word about John Chrysostom. In historical context, Chrysostom was asked to preach against heresies among fellow Christians. He decided to preach against the Jews instead on this occasion "since the Anomians impiety is akin to that of the Jews" (1.1.6). As with many episodes in the Christian drive to stamp out heresy, when a preacher wants to call out the impiety, legalism, hypocrisy, or authoritarianism of his opponent, he calls them Jews.

I have never met a Christian who was as openly anti-Jewish as Chrysostom. They are out there (as the worldwide web attests), but never in my company. I will, however, relate a story that hit me close to home.

For a short while I rented a room in the Hillel House at the University of California, Davis. The house was close to campus and in the same town as my fiancée (now wife). Davis is a little college town in a largely agricultural area of California. Lots of tractors. Lots of bicycles. The house itself was once owned by band members of The Grateful Dead. When I lived there it was occupied by four Jewish college students of varying degrees of kosher and varying degrees of personal hygiene. When I moved in, there was a poster of Public Enemy on the wall of my room, and it might still be there for all I know. It was, for the most part, just an average college guy house in need of a functioning vacuum. Little made the house stand out as Jewish save a modest sign in the front yard.

About ten years after my time there I picked up a newspaper and read that a swastika was spray-painted on the exterior wall of my old room. This small expression of hate was followed by a series of swastikas spray-painted at various Jewish sites in Davis.

I do not know how to measure the long-term impact of a preacher like John Chrysostom. I do know that the problem he helped to create is still with us.

How All of This Affects Me Personally

The subtitle of this book suggests that the author (that's me) has experienced some crisis of faith. I would not call it crisis, but I do feel a certain fear. My faith is always in flux inasmuch as it is always moving faster or slower than the rest of me. As I have said, I do not experience faith as a static thing. Faith is a constant state of motion, always negotiating the way forward. I have sometimes heard the phrase "unshakable faith." This is not something I aspire to, nor do I think it is enviable. My faith is oriented to what Paul Tillich called "ultimate concern." Tillich wrote that faith is "the state of being ultimately concerned."[17] This suggests orientation and investment in God. It does not suggest, to my mind, something unshakable. Or, in Lewis's metaphor, it is not safe.

A lifelong veteran of the highway may drive a car without a sense of peril, but as long as the car is moving the peril is ever-present. Some of us trick ourselves into believing that events will not prove fatal. More often than not, our blissful unawareness of possible danger pays off. Others are more aware of the movement all around us and feel a sense of ultimate concern; we are aware of our own mortality, and our perception of everything around us changes. And here is where the analogy breaks down, because I do not believe that there is a way to stop driving. Faith might be less like driving and more like breathing. Whatever the case, I do experience a healthy concern for my peril. But my sense of danger is not a fear of losing faith but rather a fear of God.

The times when I have sensed God most present are the times when I have been most concerned about my faith. The reality of God is an inconvenient thing when one desires a static faith. I do not ultimately trust that I will come through whole in the end because I do not imagine God to be predictable. Even so, I continue to orient myself toward my ultimate concern. Perhaps you have seen the bumper sticker that reads "God is my copilot"? What I am suggesting is that God is more like an oncoming truck on a narrow bridge.[18]

Because my faith is a fluid process, I have come to appreciate my Jewish dialogue partners, both in their Jewishness and their particularity. Because my friends typically value conversations rather than doctrinal conclusions, I am able to process my faith along Jewish-Christian borders more beneficially. (Notice here that I have used the word typically. I am aware of and concerned about my use of this language; I am using the language of stereotype here to point to my vulnerability.) Because my faith is deeply personal, my conversation partners must be particular. As self-interested as I am, I am not under the illusion that just anyone will find the rhythms and perils of my faith interesting or care to process them with me, much less reciprocate. So some manner of friendship is required for vulnerability. And it requires a Jewish-Christian border to make my specific and personalized encounters with Jewish-Christian friendship work.

> Perhaps you have seen the bumper sticker that reads "God is my copilot"? What I am suggesting is that God is more like an oncoming truck on a narrow bridge.

A number of Jewish-Christian borders have become sacred to me. A few of these are represented in this book. Here I will just say that my ultimate concern has found definition within Jewish-Christian friendship and that this has made me a more committed Christian. In order for me to continue to contribute to my specific friendships, I must continue to navigate my faith in a positive and constructive way. Put simply, in order to contribute to Jewish-Christian friendship, it is necessary that I risk the peril and remain a Christian. Honestly, my Jewish friends expect this of me.

A byproduct of this is that I have come to appreciate my internal relationships within Christianity more fully and with greater intimacy. By navigating my faith along the contours of

Jewish-Christian friendship, I have become (I hope) a more constructive member of the body of Christ.

I write these personal paragraphs in this chapter to explain how philo-Semitism has become integral to my faith. In keeping with my discussion of peril, I know that allowing anything to become entangled with my faith is dangerous. As odd as it might sound, my commitment to philo-Semitism has made me aware of a tendency that comes dangerously close to a personal crisis for me.

Richard Rubenstein's book *After Auschwitz* is still as devastating today as it was when it was first published in 1966. When I first read it, *After Auschwitz* stopped me in my tracks for about a month. I could think of almost nothing else. Rubenstein explains how very dangerous Christian theology can be. I ultimately part ways with Rubenstein's abandonment. He feels he must leave behind myth and the belief in a personal God. And I will ultimately want to nuance his portrait of Christianity. I must acknowledge, however, my debt to his book. It has given me vocabulary and definition that I did not have before. Rubenstein, in light of the Holocaust, believes that Jews must reinvent Judaism without the myth of Israel's special status.

> After the experiences of our times, we can neither affirm
> the myth of the omnipotent God of History nor can we main-
> tain its corollary, the election of Israel. After the death camps,
> the doctrine of Israel's election is in any event a thoroughly
> distasteful pill to swallow. Jews do not need these doctrines to
> remain a religious community.[19]

Rubenstein observes that after the death camps, Jews (I do not think he can speak for all Jews) embrace a renewed dignity, strength, and vitality and live within the pain and joy of the present. He seeks no "pathetic compensations" in hope for a future life beyond the grave. "It is either this or return to an ideology which must end by praising God for the death of six million Jews. This we will never do."[20] Rubenstein nods to the place of lament within Judaism. The lament psalms, for example, have given Israel sacred space to accuse God and to protest God's lack of action in the face of catastrophe. Almost all of the lament psalms, however, end in praise. Rubenstein, in referring to and then rejecting an "ideology which must end by praising God," refuses to live within that mythology. "We will never again regard ourselves in the old mythic perspectives."[21] It is possible that Rubenstein is voicing his vision for the future of all Jews. It is also possible that he refers to himself when he says "we" (as he seems to do elsewhere in the book). Whatever the case, it should go without saying that Rubenstein does not speak for all Jews.

Jewish theological responses to the Holocaust are many and varied. Elie Wiesel explored this theme through narrative in *Night*: God was among the many children lost in the death camps. In my next chapter I will explore another Jewish approach to the problem. Before returning to Rubenstein, consider these words by Michael Wyschogrod, which stand in contrast: "The human encounter with God that is expressed in praise is the one response most difficult for modern man, and particularly for the Jew, to understand." Wyschogrod wrote that, for post-Auschwitz Jewry, "There has crept into our consciousness a profound anger at God, and this anger is shared by all Jews. . . . Yet we must recognize that there was a time when men in general and Jews in particular were overwhelmed by a deep emotion of gratitude for the wonderful favors bestowed by God."[22] I offer Wyschogrod's words here only as a demonstration of the variety of Jewish theology.

Where Rubenstein's commentary becomes most challenging for me as a Christian is in his indictment of philo-Semitism. After expressing his abandonment for Israel's special relationship with God, Rubenstein observes that Israel's doctrine of election seems to be indispensable for Christians. He pinpoints an almost certain truth about Christian identity in this observation. "Unless Israel is the vessel of God's revelation to mankind, it makes no sense to proclaim the Christ as the fulfillment and climax of that revelation."[23] Christianity, in his view, requires Israel's mythology more than Judaism does. "I see no way in which the believing Christian can demythologize Israel's special relation to God without radically altering the meaning of Christian existence."[24] He then laments that as long as Christians require Israel's doctrine of election, the Judeo-Chrisitan encounter will continue to be tragic. Because the consequence is that the Christians will continue to encounter Jews and Judaism as myth and abstraction. If so, we Christians will not be able to encounter the humanity of our closest neighbors.

His statement is so close to the mark that it is worth feeling its impact even without nuance. How much of Christian philo-Judaism is informed by a "mythological Jew" narrative? And if we cannot encounter the humanity of our closest neighbors, don't we risk losing a crucial element of our own humanity?

This question is worth considering carefully. But before moving on, my quest for nuance continues: it would be more accurate and less prone to stereotype to say that *many* Christians or *most* Christians encounter Jews within a sacred narrative. Also to say that "the Christian will *always* encounter . . ." would be better said as "the Christian will *most often* encounter the Jew as myth rather than real person." But even if nuanced as such, the assessment of Christianity from the *After Auschwitz* border is haunting. It gets worse. Rubenstein argues that Christianity's mythological Jew either resembles Jesus or Judas. In the Christian imagination, Jews are either saints or sinners but there "knows no middle ground."

So even in times of Judeo-Christian friendship, Christians fail to encounter Jews in their simple humanity. If so, "another round of slaughter" is always lurking. Thus "philo-Semitism is as unrealistic and pernicious as anti-Semitism, for it destroys our most precious attribute, our simple humanity."[25]

It is at this point where I must disagree with Rubenstein. He claims that Christian thought on Jews and Judaism "extends from Jesus to Judas but knows no middle ground." Surely this must be incorrect. Christianity can be a religion of extremes, but much of Christian thought occupies middle ground.[26] Middle ground is exactly what we seem to lack when reflecting on catastrophic violence. But it is exactly what we must rediscover to meet at Jewish-Christian borders as fellow humans rather than abstract counterparts in a cultural narrative. I do not want to give the impression that I have dismissed Rubenstein's logic and no longer worry about it. His voice, although I never met him in person, continues to challenge me as much as any other voice I have encountered.

Finally, I do believe that I discover the simple humanity of all of my friends (Christian and Jewish) once intimacy within friendship has been established. So I reiterate: I have come to appreciate my Jewish dialogue partners, both in their Jewishness and their particularity. The key for my faith has been intimacy within friendship, as my next chapter explores.

CHAPTER 6

On the Border of Laughter and Intimacy

> Let us not reckon [the banqueting table of Friendship] without our Host. Not that we must always partake of it solemnly. "God who made good laughter" forbid. It is one of the difficult and delightful subtitles of life that we must deeply acknowledge certain things to be serious and yet retain the power and will to treat them often as lightly as a game.
>
> —C. S. LEWIS

> It is the test of a good religion whether you can joke about it.
>
> —G. K. CHESTERTON

Nothing Is Cooler Than Karate

My house was Italian in a way that lacked self-awareness. Some of us never learned how to modulate the decibel level of our voices. Others quietly plotted vendettas. Our passions trumped any sense of what Plato called the virtue of moderation. My sisters were fighting perpetually over a hairbrush. In my fallible memory it was always the same fight over the same damned brush. If I could propose one edit to Dante's *Divine Comedy* I would suggest a hairbrush motif in canto eight.

I was the third of six children, and dinnertime was an opera of chaos. On spaghetti night the babies would sit on either side of my father. One would eat only the meatballs, the other only the noodles. By meal's end my father was covered in any sauce that wasn't pasted to the twins' faces. Not uncommonly someone left the table shouting, sobbing, or in sullen drama. But our lives were punctuated by laughter. Laughing was integral to who we were.

I realized this long before I understood the jokes. It was the participation, the role-play that mattered. Jokes were games with unwritten rules. One person would cue a game played entirely with words. Somehow they—the adults—all knew how to play. The speaker would begin, eyes twinkling. The room would go silent as if by order of law. Sometimes the listeners were required to chime in with "I dunno, what?" or "who's there?" Other times it would just be a story—some long, convoluted retelling that was impossible to follow. What mattered was what came next: the arrival of laughter promised by every anticipating face. I could not have told you what a punch line was, but I knew that I wanted to laugh at it. Laughing meant belonging.

There was a wooden rocking chair. Of that I am sure. Our hardwood floor was feebly covered by a series of carpet fragments, each a different color. My mother had sewn them together for a makeshift throw rug. The inspiration for the project might have been frugality, but more likely it was the oddly colored 1970s.[1] I was small enough to curl my body atop one of the single, square fragments of carpet—maybe two square feet. There were adults and big kids all around the room. Relatives, friends, all were initiated in the game. I was flopped randomly on a carpet square when I heard my name. On this day one of the adults introduced the joke. Whoever was speaking said, "They say that every third person born is Chinese. Anthony, you were born third; that makes you Chinese." Then the mirthful assembly of Italians agreed with their eyes, faces, and voices. And so it happened that for two years of my life—two glorious years—I believed that I was Chinese.

Of course it had to be true. A person holding court in my living room said it with authority. He might as well have had a gavel. Moreover, no one objected. It had been settled. I was Chinese. Where's the problem? I knew that *we* were Italian. I knew with equal certainty that *I* was Chinese. (At some point I became convinced that I was only half-Chinese; I do not know how I arrived at this conclusion.)

I told my first-grade teacher. She furrowed her brow suspiciously at me before relenting: "Oh, well, I guess I can see that." I told my friends. "Do you know karate?" *Do I know karate? Absolutely!* I begged my mother for months (maybe years) to take karate lessons. I ended up settling for a karate poster above my bed. The Asian man in that poster was godlike. His jai was as white as Jesus transfigured and his belt was as black as death. His hair and skin were dark, just like mine. Nothing, my friends, *nothing* is cooler than karate.

As I grew into my family's belonging, I slowly began to understand how jokes function. At some point I realized that this particular joke was on me. It was confirmed by a heart-to-heart with my mother who took no small joy in realizing that I had been living my life in a blissful error. The dream was over.

Normally I tell this story to illustrate the fluidity of identity via intimacy. It also invites my students to laugh at my misadventures so to build a bit of intimacy in my classroom. I include it here to illustrate something more. Not only does intimacy shape one's identity, not only is this a fluid process, but humor can be integral to this process. Humor, similar to music, similar to prayer, represents much more than moments of innocuous amusement along the way. Something seemingly as trivial as a joke masks a powerful vehicle for shared intimacy.

Inside Jokes

In his masterful little book on the philosophy of humor, Ted Cohen argues that jokes are most commonly vehicles for establishing and maintaining intimacy. I can think of no topic that is nearer to the heart of my experience of Christianity but remains so liminal in theological discourse. If my Christian family (I speak now of my family of faith) did not make me laugh, I would no longer be a Christian.

I do not mean to say that I would find Christianity boring and leave for more entertaining pastures. I mean that laughter has been integral to my most intimate Christian relationships. Studying about Jesus is fascinating, and I have made a career of it. But my siblings in Christ—to borrow Paul's metaphor—are Jesuses with flesh on. Without them, theologically speaking, I could not be a Christian.

We all experience humor variously, so I suppose that not every person (much less every religious person) requires it to feel a sense of belonging. For some, however, humor can be a sneaky and profound entry point into theology. Lewis felt a connection to G. K. Chesterton's wit long before he adopted his faith. There might be a similarity here with the way that laughter can contribute to a romantic connection on a first date. Lewis wrote in a 1956 letter, "I've been much struck in conversation with a Jewess by the extent to which Jews see humour in the O.T. where we don't."[2] Laughing, at the right time with the right person, can be a prelude to new possibility.

For me it was a publication called *The Door* in the 1980s and '90s. When I discovered religiously intelligent satire, I knew that there was room for me in the church. Then it was Tony Campolo and other kindred spirits who were willing to laugh at themselves and the sacred. In my adult life, my spiritual lifeblood is infused from old friends. There are some voices in my life that represent a covenantal bond to the church; these are the very same voices that guarantee laughter.

Laughter is therefore essential to my identity within the body of Christ as it creates a sense of intimacy. Unfortunately, you learn very little about the forms and functions of laughter in most systematic or pastoral theologies. If you want to learn about laughter, you will do better in company beyond the gatekeepers of doctrine.[3]

> Laughter is therefore essential to my identity within the body of Christ as it creates a sense of intimacy.

My students who laugh at my childhood naiveté do so because children who help us see the world differently can be funny. Moreover adults, in general, like to laugh at children. But why? In some cases blunders made by novices provide the sources of humor. In addition missteps made by children are thought to be funny when they expose ambiguities in language. The joke that began my misadventure was a wordplay with the phrase "every third person born." But my misstep—if laughed at in the retelling—is of a different kind of humor. According to great Roman philosopher and orator Cicero, there is a kind of humor that does not derive from words but is funny in and of itself. Some things are just funny without words.

After the otherwise forgettable joke about "every third person born," the real joke is that I, although I am not Chinese, believed that I was Chinese and that I was disappointed to learn that I was not. Or in the words of the great Homer Simpson, "Kids are so stupid." Cicero would call this kind of humor an "of itself" sort of funny and not a verbal sort of funny. I can tell this story in any number of ways to my students and still elicit laughter. My word choices and word order may enhance the joke, but the fact of the misstep is funny in and of itself. Or think of an even more basic form: guy slips on a banana peel and looks up with a goofy grin. In this case, words are unnecessary. Some people will always laugh at this when they see it. They will laugh even more when they witness masters of physical comedy like Harpo Marx or Jackie Chan. Cicero thus makes a distinction between this kind of joke and the sort that requires a precise formulation of words like a limerick or pun.[4] Consider this example of verbal humor: the thing about German food is that no matter how much you eat, an hour later you're hungry for power.

This one-line joke, of course, plays on the old joke about Chinese food. Cohen explains how his joke anticipates several levels of common knowledge and at least one key stereotype. The audience must be aware of the stereotype of Germans who "long to control others, to have and to wield power."[5] But what makes the joke work is the formulation of words, which is almost identical to the silly adage about Chinese food. Until the final word, the line follows the same phraseology.

There is something else that makes my story about Chinese self-identification fundamentally different from the joke about German food. It isn't the length of the telling. I could easily make my little story shorter or the German joke longer. Both jokes include ethnic misidentification. So it isn't that either. The most important difference is that the first joke invites you to laugh *with* me *about* me. I am poking fun at my own naiveté in the first case. It doesn't make it more or less funny, I don't believe, but it does change the dynamic of relationships among those laughing. Some kinds of humor risk more, some less, and not every joke (even if it gets a laugh) can create intimacy.

The risk with the joke about German food is that your audience may not have heard the adage that Chinese food is only satisfying for an hour. It also risks offending those who are on principle offended by ethnic jokes. (This joke actually pokes fun at another ethnic joke, perhaps exposing a certain absurdity. It also, most definitely, plays on a German stereotype. So it may actually be two ethnic jokes wrapped into one.) There is the additional risk that your audience will simply not find this particular joke funny. Jokes that assume more common knowledge and more common sensibility will find a connection with fewer people. But a narrower audience is not always bad.

One of my favorite jokes is not a joke in the traditional sense. It is a story from my friend, Aaron Moe. Moe—as we called him in our university dorm—spent his summers mowing lawns. (Yes, there is a pun to be had here.) He did this to pay for his life as a literature student. One summer, Moe decided that he needed to make more money, and so he applied for a job reading meters. Upon answering the job ad, his potential employer asked him, "Have you ever read meters before?" to which Moe replied, "No, but I read *Paradise Lost*. I think I can handle it."

> Jokes that assume more common knowledge and more common sensibility will find a connection with fewer people.

Now, this story might work as a joke because of the various ways that one can exploit the word read. Even so, this is an inside joke. It is funny *to me* because of my fondness for Moe. Because (1) I can imagine the shape of Moe's mouth as he tells it. (2) I can imagine the smirk on Greg Peterson's face when he hears it. (3) I am fully aware that Moe is quite careful with his words—he isn't the sort to drop quips like this haphazardly. (4) I am equally aware that Greg Peterson takes special joy in a perfectly placed one-liner. (5) My wife reserves a special place in her heart for both Moe and Greg, and Sarah's laugh is intoxicating. Most important, (6) we all know that Moe (not surprisingly) failed to get the job reading meters. For all of his erudition and wit, his one-liner was the wrong thing to say in a job interview.[6] Laughing at Moe while simultaneously loving Moe invigorates an old intimacy—indeed a network of old intimacies. In sharing laughter we are reaffirming something like a covenant. With the best inside jokes we are formalizing a relationship.

In sharing laughter we are reaffirming something like a covenant.

In imagining or retelling this story, I'm reliving a complex of relationships that have been cemented in joy. I retell this joke only (until now) in certain company, and I do so because it is meaningful to those connected to Aaron Moe.

Inside jokes are among the most obvious forms of humor that reinforce intimacy. They require some kind of mutually held knowledge, memory, or sensibility. Inside jokes can call to the surface some part of a friend's identity that has been dormant or unrecognized but easily ignitable. Jokes that work with the widest possible audiences do not function in quite the same way. These do still require at the very minimum a degree of common knowledge (e.g., the literacy level required to read *Paradise Lost*). At the maximum, that which connects us in laughter requires a sense of shared humanity.

C. S. Lewis noticed something similar in relationships spurred by erotic love. According to Lewis, erotic love says, "'Let our hearts break provided they break together.' If the voice within us does not say this, it is not the voice of Eros. This is the grandeur and terror of love. But notice, as before, side by side with this grandeur, the playfulness. Eros, as well as Venus [i.e., coitus], is the subject of countless jokes. . . . Nothing is falser than the idea that mockery is necessarily hostile. Until they have a baby to laugh at, lovers are always laughing at each other."[7]

Inside jokes flourish between lovers. They are both the result of intimacy and a reinforcement of intimacy. This much is so clear to me from my personal experience that I take it as fact. What then is the function of jokes between casual acquaintances or complete strangers?

Ted Cohen likens shared humor with a moment of beauty within nature or art that compels you to welcome a friend to witness it with you. Cohen asks why we feel compelled to share a joke we have found funny: "Why do you expect me to find it funny? And just what is it you want of me, in wanting to find it funny? . . . I think what you want is to *reach* me, and therein to verify that you understand me, at least a little, which is to exhibit that we are, at least a little, alike. This is the establishment of felt intimacy between us."[8]

Cohen also writes, "When you offer your joke, you solicit their knowledge, you elicit it, in fact, virtually against their will, and they find themselves contributing the background that will make the joke work. Thus they join you. And then they join you again, if the joke works, in their response, and the two of you find yourselves a community, a community of amusement. This is what I call the intimacy of joking."[9]

Cohen observes that the hearer of the joke offers something of herself to make the joke work. She becomes an active participant in a "shared set of beliefs, dispositions, prejudices, preferences." And then, if the joke works, she amplifies her participation with a shared feeling.

An obvious example of how fundamental shared knowledge is for humor is that of celebrity impressions (what Cicero might have called *imitatio*, or caricature). For a time Muhammad Ali was among the most recognizable personalities on the planet. So for a time Billy Crystal's impression of Ali worked with almost every audience. The impression, of course, was good. But no matter how good, the impression was funny only to those who had seen Ali's flamboyant proclamations, monologues, and poetry. There is something endearing about an impression that captures something of our private experiences of public personalities. Even more important, if Billy Crystal can reframe my memories to make them more enjoyable, he has created a connection with me. This illustrates on a somewhat superficial level a sense of shared humanity. Unlike among my parents' generation, among my peers Muhammad Ali is heroic. If done well and in good humor, poking fun at Ali only enhances his cultural currency. If we can also see Ali's eyes laughing at Crystal's impression—at himself really—our shared laughter can create a sense of shared humanity. I would argue that Cohen's phrase "community of amusement" does not go far enough. Good humor can certainly begin as a community of amusement. Good humor can also create, without qualification, a community.

Consider political comics like Jon Stewart. Those of us who allow ourselves to feel anger at corporate greed, political corruption, and disingenuous media went to *The Daily Show* for something very close to therapy. We felt connected to Stewart for guiding us through our frustration to someplace darkly livable. Stewart's audience reinforced their social and political connections by laughing together. Such intimacy is broad and (perhaps) shallow. But if a good comedian can create a sense of intimacy through a screen, how much more powerful will this device be between friends? I have no real human connection with Jon Stewart. Even so, my sister and I used to take turns asking whether the other had seen Jon Stewart the previous night. We felt a need to share it, to fortify our relationship (familial, political, spiritual) by laughing at Stewart's jokes a second time together. In doing so we were reliving something meaningful to both of us by intentionally remembering it together. Sociologist Henri Bergson puts it this way: "You would hardly appreciate the comic if you felt yourself isolated from others. Laughter appears to stand in need of an echo."[10]

If certain kinds of laughter can create intimacy, it follows that humor involves risk. Why is it that I feel so deeply wounded when comedians like Bill Cosby and Woody Allen are revealed to be morally reprehensible? Why do I care more about these strangers than I do about politicians or famous musicians? Doesn't it have something to do with my sense (albeit imagined) of sharing a human connection with them? In first viewing *Bill Cosby: Himself* with my parents, I got to see my father belly-laugh until tears rolled down his cheeks. I watched *Annie Hall* with my wife early in our marriage. I cannot think of that film without thinking of Sarah. It's not that Cosby reminds me of my father or that any character in *Annie Hall* reminds me of Sarah. It is simply that those experiences of laughter were shared experiences. Cosby and Allen—in welcoming us to laugh—invited us to connect to our shared humanity. But those memories are now tainted for me.

I believe that Cohen has his finger on something important. Our desire to share humor is a yearning for felt intimacy. It is my yearning to see something of my humanity in you. I would also extend Cohen's line of thought. Humor has the capacity to establish and intensify friendship.

Asymmetrical Force

When the adult in my living room joked that I was Chinese, I experienced this joke in isolation insomuch as I didn't get it in the same way that others did. Even if I laughed (I cannot remember), my command of English idioms and polysemy was too immature to share the joke with the adult. In this example, our different cultural intelligences made us incompatible partners in that moment.

Humor, or attempts at humor, can exhibit deconstructive force when they fail. If I reach out to you with something that has struck me funny and you do not laugh, I have alienated myself in a way. This sort of failure to connect can be superficial, or appear to be. But consider the destructive force in a racially charged joke that reveals a disconnection between the teller and the hearer. If you tell me a joke that assumes my amusement at Latino speech, for example, I will probably not laugh. And in absence of laughter, will you perceive a sense of my judgment? For my part, I might simply feel sorry for you. The failure to achieve laughter when it is sought can result in the opposite of intimacy. I have called this alienation. Cohen calls this asymmetry: "Think of an anti-Semitic joke, or an anti-black joke. Now imagine the joke told in every combination of circumstances—a Jew tells it to Jews, a Jew tells it to non-Jews, a non-Jew tells it to Jews, a non-Jew tells it to non-Jews. Not only will the joke work differently (if it works at all) in different circumstances, but it may also, so to speak, change its 'meaning.'"[11]

Cohen explains that under the wrong conditions, a joke can exploit the vulnerability of a historically vulnerable group. If told from within the group, or by a member of that group, it may well achieve intimacy. All jokes, however, are conditional and require the right people, timing, voice, and so on to have a chance to connect us. Some jokes are ruined simply because the audience fails to connect with each other. In these cases the failure of a joke may have very little to do with its content or the delivery of the teller.

Think for a moment of your favorite comedic film, television show, or comedian. Now consider viewing this comedy with your significant other, a grandparent, a child, a visitor from another country. Most people, I'm willing to guess, experience comedy differently depending on their company.

I was recently told this story by a friend (thank you, Janet): there was a man who was invited to meet his fiancée's grandmother for the first time. He was warned, however, that Grandma Hilda was a strict grammarian. She was known to police others on matters of proper grammar. Sure enough, the man was at dinner when he made a grammatical misstep. Grandma Hilda, as expected, interrupted him to point out the error. Those at the table paused for an awkward silence, worried about first impressions and the impropriety of policing the grammar of a new guest. The man broke the silence with a joke:

"Hilda, *knock, knock.*"

She played along, "Who's there?"

"To."

By convention, of course, she answered. "To who?"

"Hilda, please, it's *to whom.*"

The joke worked to both allay the awkward moment and establish a connection with the grandmother. But one can easily imagine a different outcome. The grandmother might have taken the joke as a slight. Or what if she detested knock-knock jokes and refused to play along? Or consider this (very real) possibility: what if the grandmother played along, was offended by the joke, but everyone else at the table laughed at her expense? In this case, the family members may have warmed to the new member because he dealt with the grammar police in a way that amused them. It is possible that certain kinds of laughter create intimacy with some at the expense of others.

> It is possible that certain kinds of laughter create intimacy with some at the expense of others.

It is not difficult to think of other kinds of laughter that can alienate people. Most of the humor I experienced at school in my preteen years was caustic. I either did not laugh, or (worse) I laughed as a defense mechanism. Or consider an altogether different kind of laughter and one that has no intention of malice: in my college years I witnessed charismatic worship that included "holy laughter" (uncontrollable, divinely gifted laughter). Honestly, few things make me feel more isolated than witnessing other Christians worshiping in a way that I do not understand.

I do not know how much humor is asymmetrical or alienating. I would not be at all surprised to learn that most jokes fail. Much of laughter derides, masks insecurity, or feigns intimacy for personal gain. Authentic intimacy is costly and difficult. It stands to reason that laughter that promotes intimacy is also sorely won.

Seriously Funny

The theme of borders has been an important thread in this book. There is perhaps no topic that lends itself better to this theme than humor. In reaching out, we can—if we choose—reach across social borders. It matters then that we know what sort of borders we are breaching and what power dynamics reinforce these borders. And if it matters, we do well to consider the insights of a group that has reflected most intently on this subject.

That Jews and humor are often linked in America is so commonplace that the claim almost requires no support. I will, however, point out that when surveyed, American Jewry confirmed that having a good sense of humor is among the most important factors of Jewish identity. When asked, "What does it mean to be Jewish?" 42 percent of those surveyed referred to having a good sense of humor.[12] Other factors like remembering the Holocaust and leading an ethical life ranked higher, but humor ranked significantly higher than observing Jewish law or keeping kosher. Humor was almost on par with caring about Israel (43 percent). I do not know how many Christians would associate a good sense of humor with their collective identity. My guess is that most Christians have never considered humor as an identity marker.

My guess is that most Christians have never considered humor as an identity marker.

Before I say more, let me say something else about Jews that is equally true. There is a common refrain among many Jews (perhaps more prevalent in previous generations) that there is virtue in being regarded as "a serious man." The desire for one's child or oneself to grow to be a serious man has a long history in Jewish thought.

This theme was explored most recently in Ethan and Joel Coen's film parody of the book of Job. The film was appropriately titled *A Serious Man*. The film's main character, Larry Gopnick, is a Minnesotan, a Jewish physics professor living in the late 1960s. When he finds himself in personal crisis, he speaks with a series of friends and rabbis. Gopnick tells his rabbis that he wants to be "a serious man." This quest is at the heart of the film, as the title suggests. Some would argue that this quest is at the very heart of Jewishness. Rabbi Norman M. Cohen reflects on the film:

> Where is goodness, where is God, why is there not justice? Judaism's answer has always been that it is our responsibility to fill the gap: to bring order and justice and fairness and reward in an appropriate fashion. We do that by creating community and following the path of mitzvah. We do it by striving to be *mensches*. Indeed, the true definition of being a *mensch* is to be a serious man. To be a good boy! The way that we live is the center of the moral order in the universe, when there seems to exist no supernatural Deity who dishes out reward and

punishment in the simplistic way that so many fundamentalist interpretations of religion have insisted for far too long, from the time of Job to the era of Larry Gopnick.[13]

First, I love most of the films created by Joel and Ethan Coen. I love this one especially, because I am intimately connected with the story of Job. The book of Job is both sacred text for me as a Christian and great art as measured by my particular tastes. That I take Job seriously enhances my appreciation of the parody. Second, this film explores several serious (and seriously dark) themes borrowed from Job. Third, Norman Cohen's review of this film is serious in tone and concludes with sincere theological reflection. Now I will state what should be obvious by now: *this* film is wonderfully comedic. We should not make the mistake of separating what is noble, just, and compassionate in Jewish aspiration from what is funny.

Nor should we assume that Jewish humor and Jewish life are always compatible. Ted Cohen writes, "There is certainly a strain of Jewish thought that militates against laughter, that associates laughter with a loss of seriousness, with the absence of gravity." He then offers this commentary: "At its best, [this strain of Jewish thought] is a sobering, helpful stricture. At its worst, which is more common, it is a persistent mistaking of ponderousness for seriousness."[14] I do believe that the author of this proverb avoids the mistake: "Even in laughter the heart may ache, and rejoicing may end in grief" (Prov. 14:13).

I wonder if the sometimes brilliant and sometimes infuriatingly mistaken Friedrich Nietzsche encountered this emphasis on "ponderousness" in his Jewish neighbors. Consider what Nietzsche assumes about "the Hebrew Jesus": "As yet [Jesus] knew only tears and the melancholy of the Hebrew, and the hatred of the good and the just—the Hebrew Jesus: then the longing for death overcame him. Would that he had remained in the wilderness and far from the good and the just! Perhaps he would have learned to live and love the earth—and laughter too."[15]

Although he overstates it, Nietzsche rightly notices that melancholy (or better, lament) has a firm place within Judaism. He also notices that Jesus at times echoes Hebrew lament. What the great philosopher fails to acknowledge is that great lament—which is common to the human experience—can and does provide space and impetus for laughter.

Some would say that a great sense of grief is necessary for any great sense of humor. At least this seems to be true of many of the best comedians. Sarah Blacher Cohen writes, "By laughing at their dire circumstances, Jews have been able to liberate themselves from them. Their humor has been a balance to counter external adversity and internal sadness."[16] Examples of this balancing act are ancient, modern, and numerous between. One could easily purchase ten different books about Jewish humor (by "one," I refer to myself) and find that not a single joke, story, or pun is repeated. What is oft-repeated is the observed relationship between humor and dire circumstance. I will provide only three examples, all preserved by Rabbi Joseph Telushkin.

First, "Albert Einstein said, 'If my theory of relativity is proven successful, Germany will claim me as a German and France will declare that I am a citizen of the world. If my theory should prove untrue, then France will say that I am a German, and Germany will say I am a Jew.'"[17] Einstein was observing the flexibility and insecurity of the borders he occupied. Because of his fame and status, he had several possible homelands. Yet because of his

Jewishness, and because of his proximity to National Socialism, his identity was defined differently by various (capricious) external forces. Like many immigrants in wartime, Einstein was aware that the borders he occupied were quite flexible. But flexible borders can also be a source of instability. This joke is one among many that exploits this flexibility and instability.

The life of Groucho Marx illustrates the all-too-common border of American segregation alongside the all-too-Jewish border of partial assimilation: "Groucho Marx was married to a non-Jew. When their son was refused admittance to a 'restricted' country club, Groucho sent the club a telegram: 'Since my little son is only half-Jewish, would it be alright if he goes into the pool only up to his waist?'"[18]

Flexibility of one's social location is often the source of humor. But intractable persecution can also be exploited, as it is the source of insecurity. In medieval Europe, rabbis were often forced to debate Christian clergy. Too often the result of these "dialogues" was persecution (if the rabbi was too persuasive) or the expectation of conversion (if the rabbi was unconvincing). Telushkin rightly calls this a no-win encounter. "Not surprisingly, so hopeless a situation inspired its own unique brand of humor."

> In a small European city, the priest, widely acknowledged as an expert on the Bible and the Hebrew language, challenges any Jew to debate him. The disputation is to have a unique format. Each party will ask the other to translate a Hebrew term. The first party incapable of doing so will be immediately executed.
>
> The local rabbi is terrified because he knows that the priest's knowledge of Hebrew is greater than his. The Jewish community is in a quandary: they realize that whoever enters the debate will die.

Finally, a simple Jewish laborer comes forward. "I am willing to debate the priest," he says.

The debate is arranged, and the laborer is permitted to ask the first question. "What does *ai-neh-nee yoh-day-ah* mean?"

The priest answers, "I don't know" (which is what the two Hebrew words literally mean) and is immediately put to death.

The Jewish community is greatly impressed by the laborer's ingenuity. They make a celebration in his honor, and one of the guests asks him: "Where did you ever get the idea to ask the priest such a question?"

The laborer answers: "I grew up in a village near here, and the rabbi there was a very big scholar, but bigger than the rabbi here. And somebody once told me to ask him, 'What does *ai-neh-nee yoh-day-ah* mean?' I asked him, and he told me, 'I don't know.' So I figured if that rabbi, who was such a scholar, didn't know, how could this priest know?"[19]

This joke is one among many wherein an uneducated person outwits—in this case unwittingly—an elite oppressor. This type of joke is ancient and is not limited to Jewish humor. I do not know when this particular joke was first told or how ancient it actually is. What is more important is that the joke would have worked just as well in any number of historical contexts wherein Christians possessed too much religious and political power. It is, perhaps, a coping mechanism in the same way that Jewish jokes about anti-Semites can provide a pressure valve in anti-Semitic contexts. "As a rule, Jews have joked about antisemitism only when they were too weak to fight it."[20] But I think that there is something more to be observed.

Humor and Power

As I hope this chapter has shown, not all laughter is created equal. Humor can range from superficial to social commentary.

In their most meaningful forms, humorous stories allow for a rewriting of dominant narratives. If the dominant cultural narrative leaves you out, or worse, paints you as a devil, rewriting that narrative can replace a negative social image with a positive one. Sarah Blacher Cohen makes a claim that might seem strange to many Christians. She claims that humor is not simply a coping mechanism for many Jews: "It has also been a principal source of salvation."[21] These are strong words—maybe overstated—but maybe her words are strong medicine.

My dear friend Leonard Greenspoon is the editor of a book called *Jews and Humor*. This book is a collection of essays by various authors on humor in media spanning from the Bible, to medieval parody, to Gilda Radner. Leonard lays out the complexity of the topic of Jewish humor in his introduction, resisting any simple or final definition. He leaves it to the reader to decide what is commonly Jewish about the examples given in the book. If our examples range from the Talmud's laughing voice from heaven to Kinky Friedman, the self-described Texas Jewboy of country music, we will be hard pressed to discover anything decisively Jewish about Jewish humor. I do note, however, that several chapters in this book suggest that Jewish humor relates in some way to external, often intimidating forces.

Whether the power is political, social, or religious, humor is a way to negotiate the life of perceived (and often vulnerable) outsiders. This could take the form of the Marx Brothers playing with themes of immigrant assimilation. It might also take the form of remembering tragedies of the past and rewriting these stories subversively.

And now we arrive at one of the most important elements of humor in general, perhaps showcased only by Jewish jokes and comedians: laughter has subversive power. There may be no better way to protest a bully than to render him laughable. There may be nothing more subversive than making a bully laugh at himself.

Examples are everywhere and not only with Jewish comedy (although Jewish comics have been highly influential). Charlie Chaplin writes and stars in *The Great Dictator*. "Moms" Mabley talks about her forced marriage to an old man. Lenny Bruce and Sarah Silverman address the accusation that Jews killed Christ. George Carlin shines a spotlight on institutional religion. Mel Brooks writes *The Producers*, featuring the song "Springtime for Hitler." Richard Prior exposes police brutality. Joan Rivers reveals the problems of aging. Bill Cosby confesses the chaos and powerlessness of parenthood. Amy Schumer explores the evils of rape by mocking Bill Cosby.

> There may be no better way to protest a bully than to render him laughable. There may be nothing more subversive than making a bully laugh at himself.

In each of these cases—and there are thousands more—the external power is simply too intractable or systematic to bring to justice. How do you counterbalance millennia of violence against women? How do you expect to get a reprieve from Father Time? How do you get revenge against Hitler? Jerry Seinfeld concedes to Mel Brooks on this point, "There's no revenge." Brooks replies to Seinfeld, "There's no way that you're going to match him tirade for tirade; he's gonna beat you. You've got to find another way."[22]

Let us return for a moment to the book of Job. When Job finally gets what he wants (or what he thinks he wants) from God, when he finally gets to ask God to account for the mess of a chaotic world, here is what the Divine Voice says:

> Can you pull in Leviathan with a fishhook
> or tie down its tongue with a rope?
> Can you put a cord through its nose

or pierce its jaw with a hook?
Will it keep begging you for mercy?
　　Will it speak to you with gentle words?
Will it make an agreement with you
　　for you to take it as your slave for life?

—JOB 41:1–4

Three things strike me as peculiar about this passage. First, God is being sarcastic at Job's expense. I am not sure if this should trouble me or tickle me. Second, God is comparing "himself" to a mythological monster of chaos. The gist here is that God is saying, "You cannot tame me any more than you can hope to tame a dragon; I'm much worse."

Finally, and most important, from the human perspective God is seemingly intractable. How do you expect to get revenge against a moral monster like Hitler for the Holocaust? The answer is that you can't. How much more difficult, then, is it to get revenge against God for the Holocaust? Among the many things that the book of Job teaches, it teaches that the human mind has not the capacity to reason with God. Or taken another way: sometimes God just can't be reasoned with. Sometimes God is less like a righteous judge and more like something as unreasonable and impersonal as a tidal wave. Jason Kalman explains that Jewish post-Holocaust theology "does not relieve God of His responsibility for His role in the Holocaust."

The way that Kalman ends this sentence is important, and I will complete the line in short order. Before I do, I will let the fact of God's responsibility—or lack of response—sink in. If God bears responsibility for something as catastrophic as the Holocaust and God cannot be brought to justice, what is the appropriate human response? Many Jewish comedians—and they are among the very best to my mind—have concluded that God must be laughed at.

God's overwhelming power makes God vulnerable to laughter. What greater external power is there from the human perspective? Humor as a form of protest ultimately becomes a protest against God.

> God's overwhelming power makes God vulnerable to laughter.

Humor and Intimacy

I hope to have convinced you by now that reaching out to share a laugh can be an invitation to begin or enhance intimacy. It is also true that intimacy requires risk. Indeed the more intimacy we invite, the more we become vulnerable to alienation. To invite others to laugh *with you* is to leave open the possibility that they will not. To invite others to laugh *at you* is to leave open the possibility that they will see you without dignity. Any kind of humorous invitation hopes to reveal something we share in common; it could equally reveal something that divides us.

"Jewish post-Holocaust theology," writes Jason Kalman, "does not relieve God of His responsibility for His role in the Holocaust *but encourages renewing the relationship.*"[23] This is not to say that most (or even many) Jews are interested in post-Holocaust theology. And not every Jew wants to renew the relationship. But for those who do, there must be some acknowledgment that the Holocaust represents a catastrophic breach of trust.

Could it be that comedians who poke fun at God do so to reestablish intimacy once trust has been compromised? I would like to think so. For those of us who find trusting God a difficult and sometimes impossible feat, for those of us who wonder what sort of deity is responsible for what we read in the news daily, laughter at God can be something like salvation. It is like salvation because the alternative is tantamount to giving up on God's intimacy.

Nietzsche was wrong about Jesus. Jesus, I believe, did indeed learn to live and love the earth, and laughter too. Especially in his storytelling Jesus invites such intimacy. Jesus also accused God of abandonment. We should not be surprised to find both laughter and a sense of God's silence in the same personality. We should not surprise ourselves if we find both of these gifts in the mirror.

At the beginning of this chapter I confessed that without laughter with my fellow Christians I would not have created the communal intimacy required for my Christianity. I have also confessed that I find intimacy with God difficult. I am grateful for my friends (both Jewish and Christian) who have taught me to laugh at religion, at God, and at my own limitations and hang-ups. In laughter I am continually renewing the relationship.

CHAPTER 7

On the Border of Tolerance and Love

> Behold this servant of thine, fleeing from his Lord and following a shadow! O rottenness! O monstrousness of life and abyss of death!
>
> —ST. AUGUSTINE

> There is no escape along the lines St. Augustine suggests. Nor along any other lines. There is no safe investment. To love at all is to be vulnerable. Love anything, and your heart will certainly be wrung and possibly be broken. If you want to make sure of keeping it intact, you must give your heart to no one, not even to an animal.
>
> —C. S. LEWIS

The Way of Love?

Henri Nouwen described the "downward-moving way of Jesus" as a path that abandons power in favor of love. Christians, especially Christian leaders, should be "people who are so deeply in love with Jesus that they are ready to follow him wherever he guides them."[1] Nouwen suggests that spiritual pilgrimage along the way of love ought to map our social influence. The way of Jesus is the way of love.

I am deeply moved by this ideal. I desperately want to affirm it. There are two factors, however, that complicate this for me. The first is this: abandoning power in favor of love is not so simple. In many cases, love wields and maintains its own kind of power. In many more cases, power—the sort that builds ego—is entangled with love.

Second, being "deeply in love with Jesus" is volatile and can be fleeting. Some of us must learn to be Christians (and interact with our religious neighbors as such) even when God's incarnational presence is silent. What happens when the self-emptying way of love empties us of our affection for God? I have been gifted with God's silence more often than not. My prayer life is often an experience of numbness. I once thought that these were problems that required fixing. It occurs to me now that most Christian definitions of love (especially divine love) are superficial. I will also confess that my own superficial conceptions of love and God continue to create trouble for me.

This chapter invites you to process the various aspects of love with me. I realize that this process will resonate with some and not with others. I am also painfully aware that is possible to overthink love. It may be the case that we are more inclined to think about love when we feel a particular lack of it or we have been wounded by it. I have often wondered whether this is also true for theology. Maybe we think more about God when we feel a particular lack of God or we feel wounded by God. Could this be a virtue, perhaps even an aspect of grace, within God's silence?

Love and Choosing

Jewish philosopher and theologian Michael Wyschogrod makes an interesting claim about choosing to love.[2] Love can be an act of narrowing or focusing. If you choose to be devoted to your own children, it means that you are devoted to their welfare to a greater degree than others. Choosing a spouse generally means that you are electing to love that person more intensely and with more dedication than others. Choosing to love someone leaves many others unchosen. Thus the choice to love creates the possibility of "anger, perhaps even hatred." Love can be a sort of particularity and selectivity that creates enmity for those outside of the immediate relationship. "We begin to feel the pain of exclusion and ask why it was necessary for pain to be caused by love."[3] Admittedly, this line meets me with discomfort. I was brought up in the northern California public school system: we were taught tolerance; hatred was something close to a dirty word.

What did we mean by tolerance? It was always my impression that tolerance was something near to civility. We eventually baptized the slogans of "celebrate diversity" and "coexist" into our bumper-sticker vernacular. But tolerance was the original point of departure. It meant the acknowledgment of diversity and the will to suspend disapproval whenever we might feel it. There is no love story to be had here. I never once passed a note to a girl saying, "I willfully suspend disapproval of you." But if I had, I might have saved myself some heartache.

I am making light of the mantra, perhaps unfairly. Tolerance was not intended to replace love. It was meant to help us rethink our feelings when Cupid was hard to conjure. Tolerance was something of a neutral posture that could be applied to everyone. Consider one of my favorite bumper stickers: "Practice random acts of kindness and senseless acts of beauty." In my errant and idiosyncratic memory, this sticker preached from every third bumper in Sebastopol, California. It preaches what Wyschogrod might call "undifferentiated love." So where is the problem? Should not we love everyone indiscriminately? Wyschogrod answers, "Undifferentiated love, love that is dispensed equally to all must be love that does not meet the individual in his individuality but sees him as a member of a species, whether that species be the working class, the poor, those created in the image of God, or what not."

Undifferentiated love is impersonal. Personal love—devotion that goes deeper than tolerance—must discriminate on some level.[4] Wyschogrod argues that God's love is acutely personal. God's love "is exclusive because it is genuinely directed to the uniqueness of the other and it therefore follows that each such relationship is different from all others."[5]

Love is fundamentally different from tolerance. Tolerance suggests something closer to neutrality and lack of particularity. Tolerance is not without virtue. As I hope to show below, however, tolerance is not nearly as benign as we would like to believe.

Tolerance as Virtue

Love in a chaotic world comes with consequences. Worse still, because the world is chaotic, the consequences of love are often unpredictable. This real-world unpredictability is also why our repeated attempts to classify the different kinds of love are tentative rather than definitive. Wyschogrod speaks of the differences between *agape* (charity from a position of power) and *eros* (erotic love), but ultimately he concedes that these neat distinctions cannot hold up in the human experience, especially the experience of God. C. S. Lewis was also aware that the conceptual distinctions of affection, friendship, erotic love, and charity often overlap.

What all of these aspects of love have in common is the cost of painful intimacy. Tolerance does not cost the same as love. And here is where tolerance demonstrates its virtue. I simply cannot choose intimacy with every person I will encounter on my civic landscape. Not only do I lapse into misanthropic moments, as an individual person I only have so much emotional fuel in my brotherly-love gas tank. My human limitations make love on a civic scale seem impossible. A commitment to tolerance can make me a better citizen and does not demand so much that I cannot aspire to it daily.

Lewis's *The Four Loves* was very important for my development as a young Christian. It also might have been my first appetizer of the Greek language. Lewis, however, did not grow up in 1980s northern California and therefore neglected to address the mantra of tolerance. So I will rehearse briefly his treatment of the four loves, and I will add to each the wrinkle of tolerance as a possible alternative. I will suggest—perhaps counterintuitively—that there is virtue in the alternative.

Storge (in Greek, we pronounce this as *stor-geh*) is what many ancient Greeks referred to as family love or love through familiarity. This type of love seems primal, basic to human biology and instinct. I am almost tempted to tell you that you already know what this means. After all, you probably had a devoted parent, grandmother, or older sibling. Perhaps you have experienced the intense emotional rollercoaster of parenting and already know just how chaotic *storge* can be. But these primal emotions give you only a partial picture of what the ancient Greeks meant by *storge*.

It must be said the Greeks often used the words for love interchangeably. Generally speaking, *storge* is the love of parent for a child or a person in their care. The Jewish historian Josephus (writing in Greek) retells the story of Sarah, Hagar, and Ishmael and explains Sarah's affection for Ishmael. He writes, "As for Sarah, she at first loved Ismael, who was born of her own handmaid Hagar, with an affection not inferior to that of her own son for he was brought up in order to succeed in the government."[6] Sarah felt *storge* for Isaac and, for a time, felt a similar *storge* for Ishmael. This kind of affection was expedient insomuch as Ishmael was being trained to lead the clan. Those who know this story know that Sarah's affection for Ishmael did not hinder her from sending the boy away to create a better climate for her biological son. In effect, Sarah chooses one child over and against another. This is the dark side of *storge* that modern, Western parents tend not to discuss.

Storge can be used as a generic term or a term to convey great passion. Josephus also uses *storge* to describe a love of a particular kind of government[7] and the love of a close relative.[8] This sort of affection can also be tied strongly within a family network. Consider how Josephus recounts David's love for Bathsheba when their child is fatally ill: "However, God sent a dangerous distemper upon the child that was born to David of the wife of Uriah, at which the king was troubled, and did not take any food for seven days, although his servants almost forced him to take it; but he clothed himself in a black garment, and fell down, and lay upon the ground in sackcloth, entrusting God for the recovery of the child, for he vehemently loved the child's mother."[9]

As the story goes, David's *storge* for Bathsheba as it extended to their child brings a great deal of pain with it. This is a pain, I think, that almost all parents worry about. Some of us worry like David did even when there is no danger in sight. It is a feeling that is not easy disentangled from one's sense of self and from one's identity as a spouse, parent, child, and so on. *Storge* can bring with it the feeling that if it is lost, your very soul will be lost. Any parent who has even imagined the loss of a child has felt this kind of *storge*.

What this very short survey suggests is that familial love (perhaps poorly named) is wide-ranging and messy. Imagine how much less pain would have been felt if Sarah had only tolerated Ishmael or if David had only tolerated Bathsheba. Their stories might have been less compelling, but the characters within the stories might have been spared considerable grief.

Philia is what Lewis called friendship. Lewis borrows from Aristotle but could have done so with much more detail. Aristotle explained that there are three types of friendship: of utility, of pleasantness, or of virtue. The first can be found most easily in business partners. To my students I explain this in terms of housemates. Many people decide to share rent in a single home simply to offset their cost of living. It is important to maintain a sort of professional friendship with a housemate if the relationship is to last. The second sort of friendship, according to Aristotle, is "of pleasantness" or pleasure. Think here of a warm or funny personality at an office party. This is the person who makes you feel good. Or perhaps you are the warm or funny person, and people like the way they feel when they're around you. This—for better or worse—is the sort of friendship that most people seek out on Facebook. Aristotle's third type of friendship is what Lewis hopes that we can aspire to with *philia*. The third and highest form of friendship is a relationship of virtue. In this relationship both parties are mutually invested in the welfare of the other.[10] Most important, they equally contribute to seeing the other person become a person of virtue. Love of virtue is what Percy Bysshe Shelley writes of in this way:

> The third and highest form of friendship is a relationship of virtue. In this relationship both parties are mutually invested in the welfare of the other.

Thou demandest what is Love. It is that powerful attraction towards all we conceive, or fear, or hope beyond ourselves, when we find within our own thoughts the chasm of an insufficient void, and seek to awaken in all things that are, a community with what we experience within ourselves. If we reason, we would be understood; if we imagine, we would that the airy children of our brain were born anew within another's;

if we feel, we would that another's nerves should vibrate to our
own, that the beams of their eyes should kindle at once and
mix and melt into our own; that lips of motionless ice should
not reply to lips quivering and burning with the heart's best
blood. This is Love.[11]

A love based on mutual virtue does not necessarily negate
the previous two stages of friendship. Rather it brings elements
of utility and pleasure to greater completion. And such love, if
Shelley leads in the right direction, spills over from authentic
human community to "every thing which exists." So *philia* might
represent the widest range of possibilities among our four types.
But does it also include tolerance?

Even in its basest form (friendship of utility), we can see that
friendship is something different from tolerance. We may find
ourselves tolerating our housemates, but the arrangement itself is
not based on tolerance. We do not choose to live together because
of tolerance; we choose to tolerate each other because it benefits
us in other ways. Simple tolerance does not require any sort of
professional arrangement. And in this way, Aristotle might actually value self-sufficiency higher than a housemate arrangement.
(He was quite preoccupied with the notion of self-sufficiency.) If
you have never had a bad housemate, consider yourself lucky. The
rest of us know how risky a friendship of utility can be! We could
say even more of the risks of a truly virtuous friendship. To open
oneself to love of the kind that Percy imagines is to open oneself
to heartbreak.

Lewis reminds us of the love shared by a young (soon to be
king) David and Jonathan. We risk alienating our family members
and spouses in some cases for a friend of virtue. Sometimes the
friends we would die for are the very friends who hinder our ability to discern good and poor choices. Such is the case with many

gangsters throughout history. Or consider the problem of nepotism: we fail to act justly sometimes to benefit our true friends. *Philia* has the capacity to enhance virtue; it can also mask the consequences of the friendship. Could it be that tolerance over friendship can sometimes be the greater benefit to a greater number of people?

> Sometimes the friends we would die for are the very friends who hinder our ability to discern good and poor choices.

Eros is what Lewis calls in its most common form "a delighted preoccupation with the Beloved—a general, unspecified delight with her in her totality. . . . The fact that she is a woman is far less important than the fact that she is herself." Lewis—in a stroke of brilliance that probably stems from his study of medieval troubadour poetry—distinguishes between this delight and basic coitus. Basic coitus he calls *Venus*. *Eros* and *Venus* relate and overlap, but not necessarily. "Sexual desire, without Eros, wants *it*, the *thing in itself*; Eros wants the Beloved."[12] But perhaps the best part of Lewis's treatment of *eros* is the care he takes to bring out its comic dimensions. *Eros* involves not only comedy but tragic "buffoonery." If we take seriously Lewis's definition of *eros*, we find ourselves at an extreme form of selection. Erotic delight does not always focus on a single person in a single moment. But it does more often than not. The preoccupied devotion of which Lewis writes is as narrow a love as you will ever experience. *Eros* chooses—often foolishly—at the eclipse of almost all else.

Again Wyschogrod's wisdom is indispensable. Great pain can come from wanting to be chosen in this way only to learn that he or she has chosen another. But is there any less pain in being chosen? Losing oneself in another, losing autonomy of one's will, tripping blissfully into a foolish tryst—these bring both bliss and ache. Denis de Rougemont writes, "Happy love has no history.

Romance only comes into existence where love is fatal, frowned upon and doomed by life itself."[13] Of course he is right. This is why love stories with happy endings still fascinate us. This is why long-term, satisfying marriages must be fortified with other kinds of love. Indeed my parents' marriage demonstrated a mixture of *eros, philia,* and *agape.* Moving past fifty years of marriage, my parents also fortified their relationship with *storge* with six children, ten grandchildren, and several sojourning souls who found themselves at our doorstep. *Eros* by itself can be among the most discriminating and therefore among most painful loves.

This is one reason that Wyschogrod expanded the concept of *eros* to describe the relationship between God and Israel. *Eros* carries the double risk of unrequited love and requited love. And this does not even touch the unending and complicated range of emotions that derive from a happy marriage! A happily married woman was recently describing marriage to my single friend. Mark was trying his best at active listening, but it was clear that he had failed to understand what she was trying to communicate. Finally she summed it up in four words: "Mark, marriage is death." Comedian Louis C. K. has hours of material to this end. Even in a long-lasting and fulfilling marriage—one that doesn't end in divorce—your best case scenario is to watch your best friend die. *Eros* includes layers and layers of self-emptying. Lewis, like so many others, experienced this cosmic joke quite painfully. Tolerance costs so much less. Both St. Paul and some of the later Babylonian rabbis suggest celibacy in some cases. Better to expend your energies elsewhere and thus do more good for more people.[14]

Agape is a word that Lewis avoids in *The Four Loves.* Wyschogrod is happy to use this word, but he complicates it.

> *Eros* carries the double risk of unrequited love and requited love.

Wyschogrod explains that "human love is neither *eros* nor *agape*."[15] Love in the real world is a combination of *eros* and *agape*. Both Lewis and Wyschogrod employ the word charity, but concede that any attempt to describe divine love is doomed to fall short. It was Wyschogrod's hero, Søren Kierkegaard, who argued that divine love cannot be exhausted and therefore cannot be described in any comprehensive way. So I feel an acute sense of inadequacy as I truncate the topic even more.

Divine love is what Lewis calls "Gift-love." The Greek word *charis*, from which we conceive "grace," can also mean "gift." One can see the root of *charis* in the word charity. So *charis* (in Greek we pronounce this as *kar-ees*) gives us both "gift" and "grace" on the Christian conceptual map. Lewis writes, "God is love. Again, 'Herein is love, not that we loved God but that He loved us' (1 John 4:10). . . . We begin at the real beginning, with love as the Divine energy. This Primal love is Gift-love."[16]

Some have thought of *agape* as perfectly altruistic love, a gift that can never be repaid nor counterbalanced with enough gratitude. Wyschogrod writes, "*Agape* demands nothing in return. It asks only to give, never to receive." Here Lewis would agree. Wyschogrod continues, "However noble this sounds at first hearing, it must be quickly realized that it also implies an incredible position of strength. To be able only to give, never to need, never to ask for anything in return for what we give, is a position that truly befits God."[17]

This quotation is only half of Wyschogrod's point; it is not where he ultimately lands. I quote him here to show where Wyschogrod and Lewis might meet in abstract terms. Both Wyschogrod and Lewis have a sense of God's immense power and transcendence. That God would choose to love humanity at all is considered by both grace. Let us not fall into the old Christian error that the Old

Testament is just a precursor to grace! Wyschogrod's God is exactly the sort of God that we meet in the New Testament.

To the majority of Christians *agape* is going to seem infinitely better than tolerance. But those people who challenge the possibility of supernatural "Gift-love" have probably better understood the transcendence of God. A god who intervenes in the real world seems too good and too dangerous to be true. They, like Kierkegaard, confess an inability to grasp the profound implausibility of God's being and will. And unlike Kierkegaard, they have the sense to avoid tilting at windmills. Wyschogrod aptly uses the word incredible. Quite right! There is simply nothing credible about the God-who-chooses-love story. Can we really blame folks for choosing secular tolerance over what seems to be a divine comedy?

I do not suppose that any of my arguments in favor of tolerance have been persuasive. The virtues of tolerance may be convincing only at certain stages of one's life. In its ideal form, love will always seem vastly superior to tolerance. Love is simply too integral to our humanity to conclude that tolerance is a viable alternative. But I will confess that I do entertain from time to time the virtues of tolerance over and against love. I am tempted by the security and predictability of a moderate life. God's love may be inexhaustible, but humans are indeed given to exhaustion. And, truth be told, the only certainty about love in the real world is that it will expend every bit of you.

I have struggled for many years with the unpredictability, impracticality, and exhaustion of Jesus' call to love. I did not use the word impossibility here, but I might have in other periods of my life. If Kierkegaard is to be believed, love is nothing short of a supernatural gift. It takes a miracle to love as Jesus commands. Yet we are also to believe that love is both the foundation and the goal of the Christian life. I fear that most who preach love have no idea how absurd real love in the real world sounds. So I cannot easily fault those who choose the virtues of tolerance.

Tolerance as Vice

It must be said that intolerance, especially of a different religion, is deplorable. Now it might seem natural to label an evil and then just do the opposite. But while "just do the opposite" might have worked within the philosophical system of George Castanza, it will not do in this case. Just because intolerance is especially ignoble, that does not make tolerance especially noble. There is simply no moral power in tolerance alone. The man who murders puppies for sport is surely amoral. But where is the great virtue in choosing against puppy murder? No statue has ever been erected because someone decided not to murder puppies for sport. More important, some of the greatest episodes of evil are sins of omission. For example, choosing to tolerate systemic injustice is among our greatest sins. Love, according to Martin Luther King Jr., builds up the social good, drives out hate, and transforms enemies into friends. Tolerance has no such transformative power. Tolerance, in the abstract, is something closer to "power neutral." My guess is that such neutrality is simply impossible in the real world.

I do not think that I fully understood tolerance as a vice until I read Wyschogrod on what he calls undifferentiated love—what I would call tolerance. As seen above, this love is dispensed equally, not to individuals, but to species based on abstract characteristics. "History abounds with example, such fantastic loves directed at abstract creations of the imagination. In the names of these abstractions men have committed the most heinous crime against real, concrete, existing human beings who were not encountered in their reality but seen as members of a demonic species to be destroyed.

Both the object of love and that of hate were abstract and unreal, restricted to the imagination of the lonely dreamer who would not turn to the concretely real persons all around him."[18]

The chief vice of tolerance is that it must exist in the abstract and therefore has the capacity to blind us to the real-world neighbors who may or may not live up to our ideals. The same ideology created to help us tolerate one group can be used to justify the abuse of others.

My guess is that Wyschogrod—a Jewish German-American born in 1928—has a particularly catastrophic example of dehumanization in mind. But let us consider a different example: the "Red Scare" of the 1940s and '50s. The American abstract ideal was democratic capitalism. This ideal was set up against a real-world evil. Millions under the regimes of Stalin and Mao (among others) had been dehumanized and murdered. But in our ideological stance against evil—and it truly was evil—most Americans created a false god. Democratic capitalism was venerated as a form of salvation for oppressed peoples all over the world. With good intentions and with sometimes heroic measures, the defenders of this ideal created a world of false opposites. In this abstraction communists were simply evil. (Notice here the difference between the label evil versus saying that communism can create evil.) A cause meant to help oppressed nations ended up demonizing particular people. Something very similar could be said for contemporary Islamophobia. So while tolerance risks less on a personal level, it risks much more on a civic level. Slavoj Žižek writes, "It is easy to love the idealized figure of a poor, helpless neighbour, the starving African or Indian, for example; in other words, it is easy to love one's neighbour as long as he stays

far enough from us, as long as there is a proper distance separating us. The problem arises at the moment when he comes too
near us, when we start to feel his suffocating proximity—at this
moment when the neighbour exposes himself to us too much, love
can suddenly turn into hatred."[19]

Žižek is a vocal critic of both capitalism and Christian ideals
of love. Too often Christians use the Bible's command to love one's
neighbor as an abstract call to tolerance. In doing so, argues Žižek,
we are actually creating a distance between our neighbors and
ourselves. As a mainline Protestant Christian who lives among
mainliners, I can tell you that Žižek is quite right. We progressive Christians have a capacity to dehumanize one group in the
name of tolerance to another. It is often my evangelical Christian
friends—the ones who do not preach tolerance—who close this
distance. For these folks Christianity is most powerfully enacted
through personal care, witness, and experience.

Evangelical Christian missions can often demonstrate
breathtaking, real-world love that carries a powerful impact
in personalized ways.[20] I know this from experience. There is
unwieldy power in a commitment to love one's neighbor. So much
so that I often wonder if Christians should ever be trusted with
such power. Is there a way to embody the Gift-love we have experienced in Jesus that is power neutral? The answer, decidedly, is no.

There is nothing related to love (however pure) and tolerance
(however well-intentioned) that is power neutral. Both postures
can, have, and will continue to be wielded in tragic ways.

The Problem with Love and Power

Wyschogrod, as we have seen, draws out the essential connection
between charity and power. God can offer *agape* without needing
to receive anything in return, because God is powerful enough

to be self-sufficient. Many Christians will agree on this point. Lewis and Kierkegaard believed that such absolute altruism is so incredible that it is possible only in a supernatural exchange. So in order to offer authentic Gift-love, one must occupy a position of power. Gift-love, by its very nature, is an extension of power.

I hope you see the problem that this creates for Christians trying to love in the (sometimes chaotic) world of pluralism. Are we trying to demonstrate *agape*, or are we trying to demonstrate power? The two are entangled. And if so entangled, how is it possible to be altruistic?[21] Perhaps altruism is possible only in myth. Or perhaps altruism is a godlike action. If we cannot disentangle love and power, doesn't this make *agape* impossible? Lewis concludes that this impossibility is overcome only by the supernatural. He writes:

> But in addition to these natural loves God can bestow a far better gift; or rather, since our minds must divide and pigeon-hole, two gifts. He communicates to men a share of His own Gift-love. This is different from the Gift-loves He has built into their nature. These never quite seek simply the good of the loved object for the object's own sake. . . . But Divine Gift-love—Love Himself working in a man—is wholly disinterested and desires what is simply best for the beloved. . . . Divine Gift-love in the man enables him to love what is not naturally lovable; lepers, criminals, enemies, morons, the sulky, the superior and the sneering. Finally, by a high paradox, God enables men to have a Gift-love towards Himself.

Here Lewis spells out the supernatural action of God, as the Creator moves within humankind to enable us to respond to divine *agape*. In Lewis's version of this divine love story, humanity becomes something like a noble savage. Christians, he imagines, will become godlike in our ability to love. Second, Lewis believes that by some strange divine measure, humans can set aside their own interests (desire to be loved, greed for possession, etc.) to extend *agape* to other humans. "What is stranger still is that He creates in us a more than natural receptivity of Charity [Gift-love] from our fellow men. Need is so near greed and we are so greedy already that it seems a strange grace. But I cannot get it out of my head that this is what happens." I fear that I cannot get on board with him on this point. But here is where Lewis hits the mark: "Need is so near greed and we are so greedy already." Human love, even at our most altruistic, is always attached to greed in some way. Either we occupy too much power to be altruistic, or we are simply too needy.

In order for this divine love story to work, we must let go of the noble savages narrative. Humans (and especially Christians in my experience) are not immune to problems of power intrinsic to love—any kind of love. In light of the deep imperfections of Christians and Christianity, in light of our contributions to the chaos, I must part ways with Lewis's notion of pure Gift-love. I have simply not found it to be true that "Charity does not dwindle into merely natural love but natural love is taken up into, made the tuned and obedient instrument of, Love Himself."

What then of Wyschogrod? Wyschogrod's narrative is also a love story. The key players are God and the people of Abraham. To be more specific, the biological children of Abraham. It is God's special love for Abraham that demonstrates divine love for all of humankind. But it is important not to skip too quickly to the universal. God is highly selective and without any pretense of an indiscriminate, equally dispersed love to all. Israel is especially beloved. Wyschogrod knows that this will rankle pluralistic sensibilities. "But the Divine election, in its sovereignty, is of a people of

184 | NEAR CHRISTIANITY

the flesh. . . . It is the proclamation of biblical faith that God chose this people and loves it as no other, unto the end of time."[22] For Wyschogrod, God's passionate love for Abraham is the key that unlocks the central message of the Hebrew Bible.

In compelling contrast to Lewis, Wyschogrod's narrative is less about elevating the human to become a noble savage. Rather, in this love story, God becomes the savage (so to speak). Put another way, rather than civilizing humanity just enough to be able to love in a supernatural way, God inclines to become entangled in the fleshly messiness of *eros*. In this entanglement with human frailty, God mixes *eros* and *agape* to become real to Israel. God chooses

> Rather than civilizing humanity just enough to be able to love in a supernatural way, God inclines to become entangled in the fleshly messiness of *eros*.

Israel and thus chooses to love in a human way. "The love with which God has chosen to love man is a love understandable to man. It is therefore a love very much aware of a human response. God has thereby made himself vulnerable: He asks for man's response and is hurt when it is not forthcoming."[23]

The God of the Hebrew Bible becomes like a human in many ways. Is this not the God we meet in the Bible? God is possessive, at times overly protective, prone to anger, and jealousy. "God's anger when Israel is disobedient is the anger of a rejected lover."[24] God indeed suffers.[25] In Wyschogrod's story, God suffers unrequited love and revels in joy with reunion. So if I am able to borrow a term from Christian theology, Wyschogrod's love story is more incarnational—God is even more humanized and vulnerable—than most Christian theologies.

Because God is entangled with Israel in an *eros-agape* relationship, the complexity of power dynamics cannot be masked. God loves from a position of power, and Israel holds an unprecedented amount of power in her ability to wound God. These power dynamics are central to the love story. This is what Lewis fails to appreciate. Lewis's altruistic Gift-love is too good to be true. In the real world, love and power are entangled. No love story is complete without this complexity. To love is to play with something too powerful to be altruistic.

If we Christians are to take this love story to heart, to learn from it, we will have to dispense with the notion that we embody any form of altruism. As we love, we must realize that we're playing with power beyond our control. As we attempt to embody the messy (and sometimes overlapping) actions of *storge, philia, eros*, and *agape* we must realize what sort of harm our hands can do— have done. We must also be willing to be wounded in the interplay. Love often requires us to be disempowered, to become vulnerable, to become changed in the interplay with our neighbors.

I must confess my persistent (although lapsing) inability to grasp God's personal intervention. But Wyschogrod's love story compels me. In overhearing the story of God and Israel, a certain door opens for me. I have been compelled to learn more about the nature of the narrative.

A Narrative of Faithfulness

Jon Levenson, a Hebrew Bible scholar, has recently reframed this topic in his book *The Love of God*. Levenson suggests that modern readers have missed something important about the relationship (or covenant) between the Lord and Israel. Levenson challenges the notion that divine love is primarily an emotional attachment. Lovers of God, "it would seem, are synonymous with those who 'keep His commandments,' that is to say, with his 'servants.'" Levenson suggests that the love of God is equal to "the performance of his commandments. Love, so understood, is not an emotion, not a feeling, but a cover term for acts of obedient service."[26]

If we follow Levenson on this point, we might do better to think of devotion to God as enduring faithfulness rather than emotional attachment. It is only once this devotion to the divine Israel covenant is appreciated that we can begin to appreciate divine love as "both service and feeling." We should not cast aside Wyschogrod's emotionally complex love story. Rather, if the narrative of the Torah is to be followed, we must dig deeper within the story to discover that divine faithfulness (that which God demonstrates to Israel and elicits from Israel) is at the very heart of Israel's devotion. The story of God and Israel is both a love story and a faithfulness story. "No choice between love and law need be made, for in this case love and law entail each other."[27]

Alongside many scholars of ancient Near Eastern literature, Levenson recognizes that the covenant between God and Israel is (as the legal language used reveals) similar to treaties between kings.[28] In some of these treaties, a much more powerful king commits to an enduring relationship with a much weaker king. In such a covenant, to love is to serve certain needs that are spelled out in the contract. Of course, this is much different than how modern people think of love.

The surprising and perhaps unprecedented shift in Israelite thought is to make this language theological. What we find in the language of political diplomacy in other ancient texts becomes the language of theology in the Hebrew Bible. "Now [perhaps unique to Israelite thought] covenant is not only an instrument of statecraft between rulers but also the defining metaphor (or perhaps more than a metaphor) for the relationship of God and his people." Levenson explains that "the shift itself is surely of the greatest importance for understanding the love of God in the

Bible, as well as Jewish (and Christian) theology more generally, including political theology. That no human ruler can claim the same degree of allegiance that God claims; that God's kingship or suzerainty relativizes all human regimes; that all human political arrangements, even the most just and humane, fall short of the kingdom of God."[29]

A byproduct of this shift is that commands to "love those who are foreigners" (Deut. 10:19) or "love your neighbor as yourself " (Lev. 19:18) become acts of devotion to God. "The change is momentous. It means that the observance even of humdrum matters of law has become an expression of personal faithfulness and loyalty in covenant."[30] In this sense, even small acts of devotion reverberate into theological and political allegiance.

> The surprising and perhaps unprecedented shift in Israelite thought is to make this language theological. What we find in the language of political diplomacy in other ancient texts becomes the language of theology in the Hebrew Bible.

Take a moment to consider a teaching of both the Hebrew Bible and the New Testament: God's people are commanded to love. Now consider whether love can be commanded. If reduced to emotional attachment, the command to "love your neighbor as yourself" seems odd. But both Jesus and Rabbi Akiva repeat the command to love and claim that this command is of the utmost importance. It ought to be our ultimate concern.

In order to make sense of love as something that can be commanded, we must internalize the political and legal structure of the concept. It is for this reason that I have used the word devotion interchangeably with love in this chapter. Devotion better brings out the legal and political commitment as well as the emotional attachment of the concept.

Levenson admits that conceptualizing love as repeatable acts of a political and legal commitment "will be disappointing to many today."[31] Americans especially cringe at the idea of duties to a larger political system. We would rather emphasize our rights. Levenson observes, "We tend to prioritize rights over duties. We have some duties to the state (for example, paying taxes), but mostly our duties are derived from the guiding obligation not to infringe on the rights of others. In the Bible, by contrast, both positive and negative actions are *commanded*; 'thou shalt' and 'thou shalt not' are both in plentiful evidence. Simply staying out of the way of others, practicing an ethic of "live and let live," does not suffice.[32]

"Live and let live" is to my mind another mantra of tolerance. It does not, however, express the complex political and legal structure of Torah devotion. If we choose to love along a pattern of Torah devotion, love will often look more like duty. This is not to negate the emotional attachments of love. Rather, it is to realize that these emotional attachments must be attached to something more concrete.

> This is not to negate the emotional attachments of love. Rather, it is to realize that these emotional attachments must be attached to something more concrete.

As a Christian overhearing this story, I am tempted to skip ahead beyond the legal language and settle on the feelings. Evangelicals in particular hope to preach God's magnificent love in a way that bowls me over with emotion so that I cannot help but love God back. Not only does this sermon not always work; this shortcut would be a faithless reading of Scripture. Moreover, we will risk missing a key connection between the kingdom politics of God (Jesus' primary message) and love (a primary concept in Christian theology). To take Levenson's point to heart is to dwell on something that is more stable than unhinged emotions. And it is here that I take comfort. My feelings for God are fleeting. Conversely, my sense of God's intervening presence is erratic. But my devotion, my faithfulness, to God can endure when the emotional connections fade and fail.

Penultimate Concerns

BELIEF AND BELONGING

> I saw well why the gods do not speak to us openly, nor let us answer. Till that word can be dug out of us, why should they hear the babble that we think we mean?
>
> —ORUAL IN C. S. LEWIS'S *TILL WE HAVE FACES*

> I have learned over the years that theological reflection oscillates between personal isolation and communal participation.
>
> —DAVID NOVAK

Ben

One of the great blessings of my life is to have been Ben's confidant. Ben (not his real name)[1] is a retired pastor. He was charismatic in his youth, curious and bright. He was well-educated, caring, and took his calling seriously. Ben had a congregation that admired him and friends who prayed for him and with him regularly. He is also one of the kindest men I have ever met. If any person belonged in church leadership, it was Ben.

We were at a coffee shop when his voice decreased just slightly. "I want to tell you something. But I must have your promise of discretion. This is something that I've only told my wife." This was a gift. Ben had not known me long, so to trust me with what he was about to say was a risk. "It has been over thirty years since I last had a personal experience of God." He told me that he had sought spiritual direction from many different sources. He had tried to return to charismatic worship. Ben felt that he had tried everything he knew to try. Over the course of thirty years he had all but given up hope of having an edifying prayer life. Prayer had become a painful experience for him. Part of the reason that Ben retired from pastoral ministry was that he could not in good conscience fake public prayer. As he confided in me, his face conveyed his anguish in this matter. It had been over thirty years, but he was still trying, still troubled by his predicament. "I can't, with full conviction, sing many of the songs they sing in my church; the mythology is no longer meaningful to me."

Ben's story is not a story of lost faith, although many Christians might think so. It is quite the opposite. While many might think that Ben ceased to be a Christian, I know otherwise. I know Ben. I know that Ben is among the most Christian men I have ever met. For over thirty years, Ben's faith was tested. And for thirty years, Ben continued to be faithful.

Ben's trust was a gift to me, because (while he did not know it at the time) I can relate to his experience of God's silence. I often feel that my fellow Christians want me to be more certain of divine intervention than I am. I experience God's silence more often than not. I experience it profoundly and persistently. I do not doubt that others experience God with much more frequency than I do. But my guess is that many Christians are like me: *they* believe in God despite their paucity of experience. And if they are like me, they do not often talk about the paradox. If they are like Ben, they fear to talk about it and live in isolation.

I have benefited greatly from wise Christian friends and mentors. They have come alongside me and have invested in me. But in navigating my particular relationship with God and Christianity, I have benefited also from those beyond the borders of Christian faith. I realized along the way that if I wanted to take my faith seriously, I would need to learn from Jewish voices on the topic of God's silence. In my experience, these voices have greater insight on the topic.

God's silence in my life is part of my experience as a Christian. I would not want to give the impression that this book has been about overcoming doubt. I wrestle with doubt just like most Christians do. But to me that is a different topic. God's silence is not about my doubt. Rather this silence has shaped who I am as a Christian and, I believe, is a unique expression of grace.

In saying that God's silence is a unique expression of grace, I am not echoing a Jewish friend or mentor. This is not something that I'm repeating from a rabbi or a book. I don't think that any of my Jewish friends would say something like this. It is just something that I wouldn't have realized had I not journeyed along a particular Jewish-Christian border.

Familial Faith

One of the differences between the world of the New Testament and ours is that modern Western Christianity is a culture of individualism. We tend to place a higher value on free thought, self-determination, creativity, and personal rights. Competition (both in social standing and economics) tends to be valued more in cultures of individualism. By contrast, collectivist cultures tend to place higher value on the good of the community, family honor, and participation in a system that is more important than any single member of the group.

America especially is a culture of individualism as opposed to collectivism. If you have ever heard a Disney character say, "Always be true to yourself," you have witnessed an individualist mantra. If you have ever heard a Christian college student ask, "What is God's will for my life?" you have witnessed an individualist refrain. Individualist values bleed into our ideas about love, marriage, career, friendship, worship, and government. Soong-Chan Rah argues that American Christians have been deeply influenced by individualism: "The American Church, taking its cues from Western, White culture, has placed at the center of its theology and ecclesiology the primacy of the individual."[2] Emerson and Smith argue that Christians have perpetuated individualism in America: "Contemporary white American evangelicalism is perhaps the strongest carrier of this freewill-individual tradition."[3] Because modern Western Christianity is so married to individualism, we think of our religious borders differently than the first followers of Jesus would have.

I am not ready to suggest which set of cultural values is better. Collectivist cultures have virtues and vices as do individualist cultures. I will say, however, that I have been helped greatly by imagining "the Way" as something other than a religion where individual souls are saved or lost. Indeed Jesus' early community may not have been a religion at all.

The idea that a person might opt in or opt out of familial faith was not only rare; it was unthinkable to many in the ancient world. Borders were defined by belonging rather than by belief. This is not to say that belief was of little importance, just that belief played a secondary role. Abraham, Paul argues, was set into right relationship by belief (or faith). Even so, as the story goes, Abraham became the father of faith because God first chose him. God essentially said, "You and your family belong to me and we belong to each other." It is belonging that comes first.

In the world from which Judaism and Christianity emerged, borders were defined by belonging rather than by belief.

Many ancient Jews (Jesus and Paul among them) used the metaphor of family to describe their relationship with God. This metaphor fit hand in glove with their biological connections. Belief did not make a person a child of God; belief—and demonstrated belief—was a natural response to the reality of a previously established and secure belonging. This stands in opposition to what many modern Christians think of when they think of religious membership.

Religion as defined by belief is probably a notion closer to the heart of individualism. If so, what if religion had not yet been invented when Jesus was preaching about the kingdom of God? This leads to another important question: what if Christianity did not emerge as a new religion?

Imagine No Religion

In 1994 Rabbi Harold Schulweis wrote, "While there is no Hebrew word for religion in the Bible, no one would argue that the Bible is not a religious text."[4] This statement is no longer true. Some scholars now think that the Hebrew Bible was composed prior to the invention of religion. These scholars rightly wonder if there is a reason why ancient minds neglected to invent a word for religion. There is no word for religion, so the argument goes, because humankind had no need for the concept prior to the invention of the secular world.[5]

Put another way, if the entire landscape is connected to sacred narratives, sacred space, sacred time, one would not need a category called religion. But once the idea of a secular society was invented, people who had divorced themselves from the sacred world needed a new word for that which was not secular.

The concept of religion signals a distinct area of the human experience that stands in contrast to other areas of secular experience. To be religious is to choose particular avenues within an otherwise secular landscape. But the landscape of the ancient world was not secular in any way that we would now recognize. Brent Nongbri's recent book *Before Religion: A History of a*

Modern Concept has reiterated this argument wonderfully for a popular audience.[6] Nongbri leans heavily on anthropologist Talal Asad, who writes:

> Religion has been part of the reconstruction of practical times and spaces, a restructuration of practical times and places, a rearticulation of knowledges and powers, of subjective behaviors, sensibilities, needs, and expectations in modernity. But that applies equally to secularism, whose function has been to try to guide that rearticulation and to define "religions" in the plural as a species of (non-rational) belief. . . . Secularist ideology, I would suggest, tries to fix permanently the social and political place of "religion."[7]

Asad writes in reply to the classic observation of orientalist W. C. Smith, "I have not found [in eastern traditions] any formulation of a named religion earlier than the nineteenth century."[8] It is now common in the study of Buddhism, for example, to speak of Buddhist philosophy, with emphasis on the philosophical and not religious framework.

Applying this insight to the traditions we associate with Christianity and Judaism, Steve Mason says it this way: religion, as a modern category, is "isolable from the rest of our lives; religious systems may be adopted or abandoned."[9] Such was not the case in antiquity. "The concept of religion, which is fundamental to our outlook and our historical research, lacked a taxonomical counterpart in antiquity." In short, "the category did not yet exist."[10] Mason explains, "I do not mean to say that our western forebears were not *religious*. Rather . . . the various elements that constitute our religion [were] inextricably bound up with other aspects of their lives."[11]

The Bible contains many job titles. There are prophets, prostitutes, kings, and carpenters. It is rare to find someone introduced as an agrarian. The reason why we never meet Simon the Farmer or Jonah the Agrarian is that almost all common folks were farmers. Even if you were a carpenter or a fisherman, you probably raised crops on your plot of land. Farming was so ubiquitous that there was no need for agrarian as a distinct category. In the same way, the ancient world had no need for the category of religion, because the stuff that we label religious was ubiquitous.

Even in the modern world, the category of religion fails at times. In my youth I both heard and repeated this claim: "Christianity is not a religion but a relationship." I take this saying as aspirational. We repeat it because we want it to be true. A similar notion exists in the common refrain, "I'm not very religious, but I'm spiritual." One wonders if such statements serve to communicate insider sensibilities against the perceptions of outsiders. Consider this related statement—perhaps ahead of its time—by C. S. Lewis:

> The man I picture is a real Christian. But you would do him wrong by asking him to separate out, at such moments, some exclusively religious element in his mind from all the rest—from his hearty social pleasure in a corporate act, his enjoyment of the hymns (and the crowd), his memory of other such services since childhood, his well-earned anticipation of rest after harvest or Christmas dinner after church. They are all one in his mind. This would have been even truer of any ancient man, and especially of an ancient Jew. He was a peasant, very close to the soil. He had never heard of music, or festivity, or agriculture as things separate from religion, nor of religion as something separate from them. Life was one.[12]

I might make this point slightly differently. I might not use the word peasant, and I might leave room for Jewish life in urban settings within the larger matrix of agrarian life. Even so, Lewis's point is important. What we scholars have called Israelite religion is what many Israelites would have simply called life. Perhaps then religion is a concept imposed by secular outsiders onto the lives and thought-worlds of natives and native landscapes.

I do not believe that Jesus or Paul would have been able to walk away from religious Judaism as if it were something distinct from being Jewish. Life in orbit of the Jerusalem temple was not yet something that many Jews would have thought of as an -ism. Jesus

> Perhaps then religion is a concept imposed by secular outsiders onto the lives and thought-worlds of natives and native landscapes.

could choose to walk away from his biological family. Jesus could even choose to criticize the practices of Jerusalem's temple leadership. But Jesus could not choose to opt out of his Jewishness. Paul could rethink Israel's legal instruction. Paul could even choose to reimagine the dwelling place of God's Spirit. But Paul could not choose to opt out of his Jewishness.

This, of course, was the biological reality of life as a first-century Jew. But the theological dimension is also important. God had chosen the children of Israel. I do not believe that either Jesus or Paul could have opted out of God's choosing any more than a child can opt out of a biological connection.

The faith of Israel was about connectivity. It included the integral elements of connectivity to God, to biological family, to sacred narratives, time, customs, and land. One might imagine a scenario whereby an individual might sever all connections with Israel through total isolation. Again, this possibility is not so easily enacted in a culture of collectivism. To opt out of Jewishness was to opt out of life. So perhaps, we might think that death is a way out. Not so, claims the psalmist: "If I ascend to heaven, you are there; if I make my bed in Sheol, you are there" (Ps. 139:8 NRSV). Even in the grave, Israelites could not escape their relationship with God. Even in the grave, Israel's ultimate concern is ever-present.

In the collectivist culture of Jesus and Paul, belonging was not initiated by belief. God's choosing always comes first. Demonstrated belief is then an expression of gratitude.[13] It is only in religious cultures wherein individualism is assumed that it can be otherwise.

The word that Paul uses for faith and belief is the same in Greek: *pistis*. It can also simply mean "faithfulness." The more I learn about the world of the New Testament, the more I rethink religious belonging. Could it be that my belonging within Christ's body is secure regardless of my belief? If so, my individual choices have less to do with opting in or opting out and much more to do with choosing to be faithful.

Adrian

From time to time readers of my books or almost-anonymous Facebook friends contact me with questions. In many cases, these folks ask me to play the part of an apologist. They want to know that their faith is justified by historical evidence. For a number of reasons, I find these conversations less than comfortable.[14] But recently I received a different kind of note. It was from a friend (I will call him Adrian) who was not looking for apologetics. A Roman Catholic from Poland, my friend had already moved beyond questions of historical accuracy.[15] His journey had led him to a place of critical distance from the theological claims of the New Testament. But he could not so easily let go of his faith. Adrian reached out to me because he felt that the church seemed to misrepresent Jesus. He wrote that the church "totally repulses me. . . . When I attended I felt bored, childish and totally irrational." Both in how the church paints Jesus as a historical figure and how it leverages

Jesus politically, Adrian concluded that the church is on the wrong side of history. "I don't see Jesus at all in this. I just can't go to my previous faith." Here is part of my reply to Adrian:

> I don't get to choose my past. Whoever I am or whoever I become, I must come to terms with who I was. This doesn't mean I must hold on to childish things (as you and St. Paul both say). It does mean that I can choose how I relate to my former self. Do I choose to disapprove of the old me? Do I embrace that guy? I've chosen the second and I think happier option. . . . Importantly this allows me to connect to and embrace my past, but it also allows me to connect to and embrace the many and varied Christians who came before me and who stand with me now. In reciting the Apostles Creed or singing hymns, I am showing solidarity to a community of faith that is bigger than my little faith. Finally, and honestly, I'm smarter than I once was on a few things . . . but I don't have all of the answers and I need to leave room for the me that I will become. So I don't want to be so arrogant now that I won't be able to forgive myself later.

In the same conversation, I found myself writing this: "Ricoeur talks about a 'second naiveté' but I haven't been able to find this in any meaningful or sustainable way. To be honest, I've found something of a lifeline in my friendship with Jews. Jews (most) don't consider it possible to stop being Jewish. As one friend told me, 'we don't get in by belief. We can't get out by disbelief.'"

I think that Adrian makes the mistake of assuming that his inability to believe negates his belonging. It is the same mistake that most individualist Christians make and I (too often) among them. I might have argued with Adrian, quibbled over specific points of theology or historical reconstruction. But he wasn't asking for this, and I don't think it would have helped much. Rather than giving him a statement of correct beliefs, I expressed my belonging with the hope that he might find a place for himself within his own story. Or, in theological terms, I hope for Adrian to see himself as God sees him.

I have come to the conclusion that, while my identity is fluid, the ultimate concern of my life—my faith and orientation to God—is almost impossible to reinvent. For me the options are faithfulness within Christ's body or an anti-identity. By anti-identity I mean that I could, if I wanted, live in reaction to who I once was. I do not need to repeat the errors of my young evangelical self. I do, I think, have to come to peace with that person. Who I was will always be a part of who I am.

Gary Porton, a scholar of Jewish Studies, writes in an email: "I have always told my students, that unless one converts, the religion into which one is born is part of his/her identity—what s/he chooses to do with it is no different from what s/he chooses to do with his/her gender, physical makeup, economic-social environment. I have often added that true conversion is as complex as changing genders."

In my knee-jerk reply to Adrian, I realized that I had only scratched the surface of my indebtedness to Jews and Judaism. This book is something of a testimony to Christian insiders like Adrian and Ben, but it is also a testimony to other sorts of insiders who do not benefit from Jewish-Christian borders as I have. Those of us who live within God's silence—who feel it within the normal rhythms of our lives—have a greater opportunity to express our faithfulness. After all, it is easier to follow Jesus when you are deeply emotionally connected to God. On the other hand, a long and sustained experience of God's silence allows for a different sort of devotion. The devotion that I envision here begins with the acceptance of one's permanence within God's family.

Befriending

My friend Ben, you will recall, had kept his personal angst a secret from almost everyone. Part of the worry that fueled his secrecy was that many Christians would hear his story and think that he had "fallen away." This mentality assumes that there is a border of faith that, once crossed, renders the believer an outsider to Christianity. Such a border might exist, but I do not think that one can opt out so easily.

Before writing this chapter I contacted Ben to check in with him. Ben had suffered a near fatal accident and required surgery. I will give you (with his permission) and excerpt of his reply: "In the night hours after my surgery, I had a strong surge of gratitude to the doctors, the nurses, my wife, and Someone More. It was the first time in many years I did have a sense of a personal gratitude within the universe and even to the universe. I interpreted this experience as allowing me to reaffirm my belonging to the faith community worshiping a personal Creator God, with some sense of personal integrity."

I do not include this to suggest a happy ending. Life with God is always more chaotic than can be found in stories with happy endings. Ben renewed his efforts to experience God and continued trying for several months. He writes that his "worldview pendulum has ceased its wide swings and has slowed now to a slight undulating between affirmation and doubt but from within the Christian community."

I include this follow-up to Ben's story to argue for a longer and broader view of Christian belonging. I lament with Ben that his community of faith would not (and in some cases did not) have a place for him. I lament that he had to suffer quietly for thirty years for fear of what his expression of belief would have cost to his status of belonging. And I lament for his entire community of faith.

I believe that Ben could have taught them a great deal about faithfulness. Surely he wasn't the only one who had remained silent about God's silence.

Ben and his community would have benefited (I am convinced) from a more familial view of faith. The mentality that requires the Christian to continue to express the correct beliefs about our transcendent and ultimately ineffable God or else face outsider status is far too individualistic. Familial faith is stronger than this. As my friend Gloriajean Wallace recently preached, "Sometimes when you lose nearly everything, including your own self-identity, you need a little encouragement. Have you ever been there? Does anybody here know what I'm talking about? Sometimes you need somebody else's faith to hold on to so that you don't lose all of yours."[16]

This, I believe, is where journeying along Jewish-Christian borders can most benefit the Christian. My friend Larry Behrendt recently told me of a conversation he had with a Christian on a bus. The Christian asked Larry why he, a Jewish intellectual, was invested in dialogue with Christians. Larry's investment in Christian well-being is complex, but one of the things that came out of the conversation was this:

> I think Christians can say things to me that they can't say to other Christians, because there's nothing a Christian can say to me that would cause me to wonder whether they really are Christian. They can harbor doubts, or hold beliefs that don't measure up to this or that creed, and they're still fully Christian to me. This doesn't exactly work in reverse in my experience: because I was born of a Jewish mother, my Jewishness is not in doubt. But other Jews will question the Jewishness of my Judaism, and Christians don't do that. So there are things I can say to my Christian dialogue partners that I can't comfortably say to other Jews.

Amy-Jill Levine teaches classes in New Testament and Judaism at Vanderbilt University. As she says, Nashville is something like "the buckle of the Bible Belt." As such, many of her students are Christians. And as Levine is quite forthright about her Jewishness, many of the Jewish-Christian borders in her classrooms are exposed and discussed openly. She is candidly invested in Jewish well-being; she is also candidly invested in the well-being of her students, Christian or otherwise. "I make sure that nobody loses their faith in my classroom," she tells me. It is also common for her Christian students to come to her for advice and consolation when their faith is being challenged on campus.

In her book *Life on the Fringes,* Haviva Ner-David writes of the necessity of doubt in her spiritual journey. After reading *The Diary of Anne Frank* and *Night,* Ner-David writes, "I lost the faith that I had in a just world with a just God watching over us. Without such a God, life looked much more frightening. My eyes were opened to the realities of a world with evil. In the absence of the God of my childhood, the God who was described to me in Jewish day school, the God who punishes the wicked and rewards the righteous, the God who cares about what we eat and wear and say, what would fill that void? . . . I did not know if there was a God, but I did know that even if there was, this was not a God that I trusted."

Ner-David writes of her steps away from her childhood faith. "It was a step away from observant Judaism that would eventually lead me back again."[17] There is a Jewish-Christian difference here that must be emphasized. Haviva Ner-David was able to take very personal steps away from her childhood within the security of her Jewishness. Her familial belonging to Jewishness allowed for a personal journey away from and back to Judaism. "Actually, I realized that no matter how far I tried to run, I could never escape that essential part of myself. Judaism was too integral a part of my identity and my soul for me to be able to cast it off."[18]

My hope is for more Christians to understand that belonging is bigger than believing. On this point, I experience what Christian scholar Krister Stendahl called, "holy envy."[19]

Belonging

Richard Rubenstein, to whom I referred previously in this book, writes from the perspective of what might be called a demythologized Judaism. Rubenstein argues that Christianity cannot be demythologized in the same way, and I agree with him on this point. I also appreciate his view on the "facticity" of belonging:

> No one chooses the community, the nation, or the tradition to which he is heir at birth. There is an absurd facticity, not only to our modes of finding ourselves in the world, but to the ways in which we are thrust into our respective religious situations. Neither Jew nor gentile is entirely free to confront God's mysterious singularity as if no one had preceded him. Jew and gentile alike are thrown into historically, culturally, psychologically and religiously defined situations which are, in a certain sense, beyond choice.[20]

So, then, if a person cannot change how we are thrown into our specific histories, traditions, cultures, and times, can any person truly deny the religion or nationality of their birth or choose to abandon it for another? He answers, "We can, if we want, deny them, but this denial will be dialectically related to the original fact of the givenness of our traditions."[21] I can embrace my identity and use it as a launching point, or I can choose an anti-identity whereby I simply reflect my past in negative relief. Rubenstein hits the mark when he writes, "There is no way for the

Christian to confront the holiness of God save through the Christ and the paths of sanctity in which He is the decisive figure." This represents for the Christian what Paul Tillich names the "ultimate concern" of the Christian. But, somehow, I hear this with different impact when I receive it from Rabbi Rubenstein. As a Christian, my ultimate concern was something that was elected for me long before I was aware of it.

This realization is challenging but ultimately comforting. I take comfort here because I have a bit of "rabbit in my blood," as the Captain from *Cool Hand Luke* calls it. From time to time I have felt a strong urge to run from God. I do not experience the rabbit often anymore, but it's there, part of me. If I am honest, I sometimes feel like a coward for not running more often. Most of the time I am grateful for a realization that I have internalized along Jewish-Christian borders: running from God is an interesting plotline, but tends to arc toward return in most cases.

In my comings and goings along Jewish-Christian borders I have learned about religious asymmetry, the relationship of truth to power, friendships of virtue, the awesome and awful silence of God, the shadows cast by Christian failure, the need for collective repentance, the consequences of a low Christology, and more. The realization most precious to me relates to my sense of belonging. I can choose my steps, but I cannot choose the landscape of my life with God. I have decided to appreciate these contours and borders rather than attempting to overcome them.

Afterword

ROOTS

The day before I met Ali Abu Awwad I was in Nazareth. I try not to be cynical, but I was swimming in cynicism that day. I had been to biblical site after site designed to capitalize on my connection to Jesus. Topping the Mount of Precipice represented the pinnacle of my disappointment with Israel. Whatever else we are, Christian pilgrims are believers. Many of Israel's tourist attractions rely on this fact. Sometimes we want to believe the supernatural so fervently that we invent it.

Tradition holds that this hilltop represents the place where an angry mob attempted to kill Jesus (Luke 4:28–30). The Mount of Precipice is just one example of how a tradition commemorated hundreds of years after the life of Jesus can become a holy site. This place, like so many others, was made sacred sometime between fourth-century pilgrimages and the medieval crusades. The website jesustrail.com explains that this hilltop has become legendary: "One local legend says that the cave opened up to hide Jesus from the angry mob. Another tradition says that Jesus leapt from the mount, landing 9 km away on Mt. Tabor, hence the Arabic name for the mount, *Jebel Qafzeh*, which translates to 'mount of the leaping.'"[1]

Another webpage explains that Jesus jumped off the hilltop and disappeared.[2] The plaque at the physical site simply says that Jesus leapt to escape the mob. Luke 4:30 reads, "But he walked right through the crowd and went on his way."

I do not think that this story in Luke 4 intends to convey anything supernatural. But the legend is now superimposed onto the landscape to enhance our spiritual connection to it, reinforcing a sense of sacred identity. Yet again I sense my distance from the typical Christian experience. I feel small, isolated, unable to connect to the legend as so many others have. This time the faith of millions of pilgrims and a history of faith is of no comfort.

Nazareth is filthy with trash. As our group winds around the hills that encompass the city, we notice that the public spaces are littered with old appliances, tires, mattresses, and all kinds of debris. Here you can visit one of the most breathtaking buildings in the world. The Basilica of the Annunciation represents layers upon layers of church tradition, sacred relics, medieval art, and modern architecture. In order to get to this holy site, you must trek through largely Muslim neighborhoods and witness the poor living conditions of so many Arabs in Israel. I feel debilitated by the complexity here.

My guide, a personal friend and Orthodox rabbi, tells me that "it's more complicated than we know." He's right. But I have no confidence that my pilgrimage here is helping matters. America's fingerprints are all over the landscape. Along the highway, two billboard ads stand side by side: one features a grotesquely thin, blonde model selling perfume; the other features Santa Claus selling sunglasses.

Later in the day we boat across Galilee to our five-star hotel in Tiberias. On the water where Jesus rebuked the storm, our guides crank up the contemporary American Christian music on the boat's stereo system. Our guides are not Christians themselves; it is simply their job to know what sort of music American Christians enjoy. They give us the worship experience we came for. Others in my group worship and experience God here on the water. I cannot stand the tourism of it. But I do my best to hold my tongue. Who am I to ruin the worship of others? I retreat to my interior and remember my experience in Nazareth. The squalor and sacred spaces of Nazareth haunt me.

The next day poured a kind of rain unseen on any Sunday school flannel board. Our tour bus took an alternate route south to avoid potential flooding. My group of seminarians stepped off the bus down to a gravel driveway, holding our hoods close to our faces against the wind. We walked and ran at various speeds to shelter. It was a shack with a secure roof and a woodstove in the center. The walls were constructed of castoff materials. An old door, horizontal fence posts, polyurethane, blankets. The gaps between the materials let in the daylight. These walls modestly restrict most of the weather. As we encircled the woodstove Rabbi Hanan Schlesinger welcomed us.

"How is it that I have lived here for thirty years and never met a Palestinian until two years ago?" he began. Rabbi Schlesinger told his story about living in the Land as he believed was his religious obligation and most life-giving commitment. I bristled at the first five minutes of his talk. It sounded too much like pro-Zionist propaganda. Again, I held my tongue.

Historically, Jews lived north and south of Jerusalem. We lived in what is called today the West Bank. When Israel conquered the West Bank in 1967, it—from my perspective—opened the gate for Jews to come back to the place where Abraham, Isaac, and Jacob walked, where David ruled, where the miracle of Hanukkah happened, to our ancient homeland. There can be nothing more powerful and more significant than that. I thank God that I live in this generation. It is what my medieval ancestors prayed for but never saw.

For all my rants against stereotypes I found myself in error once again. Rabbi Schlesinger shared how his life as a settler had changed two years ago when he realized that his own "partial truths" about Palestinians had misguided him for almost three decades. "A falsehood is a partial truth masquerading as a complete truth." As a Jewish settler on the West Bank, he simply could not see the truth of Palestinian suffering as a result of Israeli occupation. Specifically, he confessed that he had persistently failed to recognize the humanity of his non-Jewish neighbors. Schlesinger continued:

> [A]nd I believe that the truth and the righteousness of that story have blinded me to another truth, to another people. I lived for over thirty years in Judea and I never saw the Palestinians. It was as if they didn't exist. . . . In 1948, when six hundred thousand Jews declared a third Jewish commonwealth, and now we have a Jewish homeland, we have refuge for Jews around the world after the Holocaust, we didn't notice that our victory constituted a tragedy for another people. We just didn't see the Palestinians. We didn't see the Palestinian diaspora that we were creating.

Rabbi Schlesinger spoke with passion and compassion about how his Judaism has since been enhanced by Muslim friendship. "Now my truth is being supplemented by Palestinian truth." He then introduced Ali Abu Awwad.

Awwad is a Palestinian, a former militant, and the cofounder of Roots. His story includes the brutal death of his brother, a debilitating gunshot wound, torture, and four years in an Israeli prison. He spoke of an event in prison that changed his life. He and his mother were in separate prisons and wanted to see each other. They both undertook a hunger strike that lasted seventeen days. He recounts, "My mother and I succeeded in something for the first time in our lives in Israel. That event changed my life. For the first time I could see the power of my own humanity. I made my enemy give up by acting nonviolently. By creating a secure place for my enemy to see me as a human being, to recognize my rights, I finally had success. It was through nonviolent demonstration that I became the best fighter for my rights. When we act nonviolently, we celebrate our existence."

Awwad is now devoted to the study of peace activism, including the lives of Gandhi, Martin Luther King Jr., and Nelson Mandela. This devotion is an extension of his life as a Muslim. Awwad and Rabbi Schlesinger demonstrate authentic friendship. They talk with pain and discomfort using words like occupier, settler, right-wing extremists, torture, hate, desperate. They also laugh together. Their jokes reveal a deep understanding of their precarious circumstance. Awwad explains that interreligious dialogue is not about agreement. "It is about creating a secure place for argument." He also tells me that becoming a peace activist is not about being passive; "It is about becoming an artist of my own humanity."

Here in this shack, I have met a Jew and a Muslim devoted to creating peaceful and mutually beneficial borders. One member of our group asks, "What can Americans do to help?"

"Come visit us before you judge us," Awwad answers. "I believe that well-informed Christians can be a bridge between Muslims and Jews. We need your understanding and help, not your M-16s." I cannot help but doubt that American Christians will seek the nuance required to build bridges. But Ali Abu Awwad's faith in Christians inspires me.

As I reflect on Awwad's bridge metaphor I am reminded of a diagram I use for my New Testament classes. The diagram shows a vertical line that connects humanity to God. It also shows several vertical lines that connect God to all of Creation. Finally, the diagram includes several horizontal lines. These represent the relationships that humans have to each other, to the Land, and to the Cosmos. I use these lines to chart a divine web of relationships. No relationship, no connection is isolated. Our horizontal stewardship of the earth affects our vertical life with God. Our vertical life of worship affects our horizontal human bridges.

In this shack, in meeting Awwad and Schlesinger, I have made two horizontal connections. I also believe that these meetings represent something more, something vertical. I believe that God was present in that mishmash shelter, the wind whistling through the horizontal gaps in the walls.

—JANUARY 13, 2016, THE OLD CITY,
THE CHRISTIAN QUARTER

To learn about and donate to Roots, visit:
www.friendsofroots.net/

Acknowledgments

This book is unlike anything I've attempted before. It is more personal and required a different sort of advice and mentorship than my work as a historian or student of sacred texts. I am always grateful that any friend, colleague, or family member would take the time to advise me on a chapter. But I am especially grateful for the eyes that looked at this book and the insights that came back. I imagine that offering feedback on a work of personal reflection can be tricky. The following names represent important and generous voices. Some read full chapters; others participated in meaningful conversations: Peter Bellini, John Castelein, Michael Cook, Katya Covrett, Damien Cyrocki, Lisa Hess, Brad Hirschfield, Gary Le Donne, Lisa Le Donne, Matthew Levering, Amy-Jill Levine, Brian Phipps, Gary Porton, Christopher Simpson, Henry Suhr, Gloriajean Wallace, and Nathan Young. Any missteps I've made are mine and probably could have been avoided if I had listened to these folks more carefully.

I am also grateful for the friendships of Larry Behrendt, Chris Keith, Sarah Le Donne, Joel Lohr, Edward Peacock, and Barry Schwartz. They have fingerprints on many of these pages, even when not explicitly named or called out in an endnote. Leonard Greenspoon may well be the kindest person on the planet. His foreword to this book is thoughtful, funny, and erudite, all in keeping with his reputation!

This book is dedicated to my mother, Patricia Le Donne. She is great in all the ways a mother should be great. But in dedicating this book to her, I am thinking specifically of her love of books. She grafted her bookishness onto me by reading to me about Gerald the Third, David and Goliath, Bilbo Baggins, and Lucy Pevensie. Thank you, Mom.

Notes

Introduction

1. C. S. Lewis, *Mere Christianity* (New York: Macmillan, 1956), vi.

2. Unlike most books conversant with Lewis, I am much less interested in Lewis's central claims or his essential theory/philosophy/theology. For example, in his helpful essay "On Theology," Paul Fiddes demonstrates an interest in a theological "centre" or "heart." Fiddes writes, "Lewis has excellent theological instincts [in his *Beyond Personality*]. If one is looking for the heart of Christianity, for 'mere Christianity', this is right on target. He has anticipated a great deal of modern Christian doctrine . . ." Fiddes also writes that Lewis' doctrines of God, human nature, and salvation—while at times disturbing—concisely "hit the very centre of Christian belief. . . ." (*The Cambridge Companion to C. S. Lewis* [Cambridge: Cambridge Univ. Press, 2010], 89–103, here 89–90). I think that Fiddes naturally reflects the chief interest of most readers of *Mere Christianity*. The "target" is essential doctrine. It is not, however, the target of this book.

3. C. S. Lewis, foreword to *Smoke on the Mountain: An Interpretation of the Ten Commandments*, by Joy Davidman (Philadelphia: Westminster, 1953), 8.

4. Ibid., 7–8.

5. Davidman's son writes, "They both came to Christ via the long and difficult road which leads from Atheism, to Agnosticism, and thence by way of Theism finally to Christianity." ("Introduction," in C. S. Lewis, *A Grief Observed* [New York: Harper Collins, 1994], xvii).

6. See, e.g., Stanley N. Rosenbaum ("Our Own Silly Faces: C. S. Lewis on Psalms," accessed November 2015, www.religion-online.org/showarticle .asp?title=1684), who writes, "Apparently, Lewis's chief informant on Judaism is Joy Davidman, his formerly Jewish wife, whose attitude toward the religion she left could charitably be described as poisonous."

7. C. S. Lewis, *Reflections on the Psalms* (New York: Harcourt, Brace, and Company, 1958), 71. What Lewis fails to say here is that it is often the Christians who are the bullies, lascivious, cruel, dishonest, spiteful, and so forth—and it is often the Christians who incite these qualities in others.

8. Lewis, *Mere Christianity*, 33.

9. Ted Cohen, *Jokes: Philosophical Thoughts on Joking Matters* (Chicago: Univ. of Chicago Press, 1999), 65–66.

10. Ibid., 66.

11. Amy-Jill Levine, "Jesus in Jewish-Christian Dialogue," in *Soundings in the Religion of Jesus: Perspectives and Methods in Jewish and Christian Scholarship* (Minneapolis: Fortress, 2012), 185.

12. I say here that we are "close to the mark." But no cigars are likely to be awarded for this description of Judaism. I have also used the term religion but this description doesn't quite work either (although many Jews would be happy with it). To be more accurate, we should probably think of Judaism as a "memory community." As such, Jewish identity involves family memories, remembering lineage, remembering the Holocaust, remembering the exodus, etc.

13. David Nirenberg, "The Rhineland Massacres of Jews in the First Crusade: Memories Medieval and Modern" in *Medieval Concepts of the Past: Ritual, Memory, Historiography*, eds. Gerd Althoff, Johannes Fried, Patrick J. Geary (Cambridge: Cambridge Univ. Press, 2002), 279–309.

14. Eric Marcus, *Making Gay History: The Half-Century Fight for Lesbian and Gay Equal Rights* (New York: HarperCollins, 2002), 19–70.

Chapter 1: On the Border of Pilgrim and Stranger

1. In some Jewish traditions, counting people is frowned upon. I am aware that by making this point, I risk offense. Nonetheless I feel that it is an important point.

2. I have since learned that some churches do employ armed guards and that these guards are hidden from view, often with concealed weapons.

3. "Suspect in Kansas Shootings a Longtime Anti-Semite, Group Says," *Chicago Tribune*, April 14, 2014, http://www.chicagotribune.com/news/chi-kansas-jewish-community-shootings-20140413-story.html.

4. The Greek word for apostle literally means "sent one."

5. For more on this theme, see Julia Bolton Holloway, *The Pilgrim and the Book: A Study of Dante, Langland and Chaucer* (New York: Peter Lang, 1992).

6. Josh Nathan-Kazis, "Poll: 81% of Jews Back Gay Marriage," *The Forward*, April 3, 2012, http://forward.com/opinion/154171/poll-81-of-jews-back-gay-marriage/.

7. C. S. Lewis, *Surprised by Joy* (New York: Harcourt, 1955), 8–9.

8. Gutiérrez writes: "The unqualified affirmation of the universal will of salvation has radically changed the way of conceiving the mission of the Church in the world. It seems clear today that the purpose of the Church is not to save in the sense of 'guaranteeing heaven.' The work of salvation

is a reality which occurs in history. . . . The Church must cease considering itself as the exclusive place of salvation and orient itself toward a new and radical service of people. Indeed, the Church of the first centuries lived spontaneously in this way. Its minority status in society and the consequent pressure that the proximity of the non-Christian world exercised on it made it quite sensitive to the action of Christ beyond its frontiers, that is, to the totality of his redemptive work"; Gustavo Gutiérrez, *A Theology of Liberation*, 15th Anniversary Edition, trans. Caridad Inda and John Eagleson (Maryknoll, NY: Orbis, 1988), 143–44. I should also add that Gutiérrez is not consistent on this matter and at times displays anti-Jewish tendencies. My thanks to Amy-Jill Levine for pointing this out.

9. Quoted from Gayraud S. Wilmore, *Black Religion and Black Radicalism: An Interpretation of the Religious History of African Americans*, 3rd ed. (Maryknoll, NY: Orbis, 2002), 249.

10. Frances M. Young, *Brokenness and Blessing: Towards a Biblical Spirituality* (Grand Rapids: Baker, 2007), 59.

11. This is an excerpt of a longer conversation that took place over several days, over dinner, in a public forum, and via email. My thanks to Lisa Hess and Brian McGuire for hosting. My thanks to Brad for allowing me to include his insights.

12. Henri J. M. Nouwen, *In the Name of Jesus: Reflections on Christian Leadership* (New York: Crossroad, 1989), 82–84.

Chapter 2: On the Border of Always Winter and Always Christmas

1. Rabbi Brad Hirschfield shared this with me via personal conversation during our trip to Israel/Palestine.

2. Christians, of course, also range widely on any number of issues. Those of us outside of the Roman Catholic communion also have no pope. The key difference here is that many Christians pursue finality. Some of us see particular virtue in narrowing the conversation rather than broadening it.

3. C. S. Lewis, *God in the Dock* (Grand Rapids: Eerdmans, 1970), 61.

4. "Veni, Veni Emmanuel; O Come, O Come, Emmanuel," accessed December 2015, http://www.preces-latinae.org/thesaurus/Hymni/VeniEmm.html.

5. The gospels Mark, Luke, and John all use exodus imagery too. I refer here to Matthew because it uses the exodus most explicitly in Jesus' birth narrative.

6. James O. Young and Susan Haley, "'Nothing Comes from Nowhere':
Reflections on Cultural Appropriation as the Representation of Other
Cultures," in *The Ethics of Cultural Appropriation*, ed. James O. Young and
Conrad G. Brunk (Oxford: Wiley-Blackwell, 2009), 1–10, here 1.

7. A survey conducted in 2013 suggests that while 90 percent of Americans
celebrate Christmas in some way, only 9 percent celebrate Advent.
Joanna Piacenzahttp, "War on Christmas? Merry Christmas vs. Happy
Holidays," last modified December 14, 2015, accessed December 2015,
http://publicreligion.org/2015/12/war-on-christmas-merry-christmas
-vs-happy-holidays/.

8. "Internet Evangelist Says Starbucks' Holiday Cups Are Red Because They
'Hate Jesus,'" *Fox News*, November 9, 2015, http://www.foxnews.com/leisure
/2015/11/09/internet-pastor-starts-merrychristmasstarbucks-movement/.

9. "Donald Trump: 'Maybe we should boycott Starbucks,'" CNN Politics,
November 10, 2015, http://www.cnn.com/2015/11/09/politics/donald
-trump-starbucks-boycott-christmas/.

10. Mark I. Pinsky, *A Jew among the Evangelicals: A Guide for the Perplexed*
(Louisville: Westminster John Knox, 2006), 55.

11. C. S. Lewis, *The Joyful Christian: 127 Readings* (New York: Touchstone,
1977), 203–5.

12. http://videos.nymag.com/video/Jon-Stewart-Rips-Into-FOXs-War;
accessed November 2015.

13. Larry Behrendt, "Greetings 101," *Jewish-Christian Intersections* (blog),
December 4, 2014, http://jewishchristianintersections.com/?p=745.

14. Franklin Graham, "The War on Christmas Is a War on Christ," *Decision
Magazine*, November 25, 2014, http://billygraham.org/decision-magazine/
december-2014/the-war-on-christmas-is-a-war-on-christ/.

15. Behrendt, "Greetings 101."

16. C. S. Lewis, *The Lion, the Witch and the Wardrobe* (New York:
HarperTrophy, 1978), 114–17.

17. To play up further the contrast between Father Christmas and the witch,
consider this: the witch offers a false gift, Turkish delight. This is a "gift"
that takes more from Edmond than it promises. On the other hand, the
historical St. Nicholas (upon whom Father Christmas is based) was the
Bishop of Myra, which is located in modern-day Turkey. So in contrast
to the witch who promises Turkish delight, Father Christmas is himself a
delightful fellow from Turkey. Given the Turkish connection, it may also be
relevant that Lewis names the White Witch "Jadis." The word for witch in
Turkish is *cadı*, pronounced, *jah-duh*. Aslan, in Turkish, means "lion." (My
thanks to folklorist and friend Nathan Young for his help.)

Chapter 3: On the Border of Jesus and Genocide

1. It may well be that a pregnant silence is the least inappropriate of all responses. Silence, however, cannot be pregnant if it fails to inform and engender ongoing conversation. See Pinchas Peli, "In Search of Religious Language for the Holocaust," *Conservative Judaism* 32, no. 2 (1979): 3–24.

2. John Rousmaniere, *A Bridge to Dialogue* (New York: A Stimulus Book, 1991), 54.

3. I believe that every Christian who can should read Susannah Heschel's *The Aryan Jesus* (Princeton: Princeton Univ. Press, 2008).

4. Pew Research Center, "A Portrait of Jewish Americans," October 3, 2013, http://www.pewforum.org/2013/10/01/jewish-american-beliefs-attitudes -culture-survey/.

5. Arieh Doobov, *The Vatican and the Shoah: Purified Memory or Reincarnated Responsibility?* (Jerusalem: Institute of the World Jewish Congress, 1998), 8.

6. Progressive mainliners have a different approach, equally problematic, that I will discuss later.

7. My gratitude to Larry for allowing me to reproduce this dialogue here. It is a dialogue that Larry and I recorded and transcribed.

8. *Rimshot.*

9. Fred R. Shapiro, *The Yale Book of Quotations* (New Haven: Yale Univ. Press, 2006), 148.

10. Michael J. Cook, *Modern Jews Engage the New Testament: Enhancing Jewish Well-Being in a Christian Environment* (Woodstock, VT: Jewish Lights, 2012), 4.

11. Anti-Defamation League, "Passion Plays in History and Theology," June 24, 2003, http://archive.adl.org/interfaith/passion_theology.html.

12. Collin Hansen, "Why Some Jews Fear the Passion," *Christianity Today*, August 8, 2008, http://www.christianitytoday.com/ch/news/2004/feb20. html.

13. As quoted from V. George Shillington, *Jesus and Paul before Christianity: Their World and Work in Retrospect* (Eugene, OR: Wipf and Stock, 2011), 11. For a fuller context of Hitler's quotation, see Helena Waddy, *Oberammergau in the Nazi Era: The Fate of a Catholic Village in Hitler's Germany* (Oxford: Oxford Univ. Press, 2010), esp. vii; chap. 1.

14. In 2000, a group of 220 Jewish rabbis and scholars signed a statement called *Dabru Emet* (lit. "speak the truth"). On the topic of Christianity's role in the Holocaust, they write: *"Nazism was not a Christian phenomenon.* Without the

long history of Christian anti-Judaism and Christian violence against Jews, Nazi ideology could not have taken hold nor could it have been carried out. Too many Christians participated in, or were sympathetic to, Nazi atrocities against Jews. Other Christians did not protest sufficiently against these atrocities. But Nazism itself was not an inevitable outcome of Christianity. If the Nazi extermination of the Jews had been fully successful, it would have turned its murderous rage more directly to Christians. We recognize with gratitude those Christians who risked or sacrificed their lives to save Jews during the Nazi regime. With that in mind, we encourage the continuation of recent efforts in Christian theology to repudiate unequivocally contempt of Judaism and the Jewish people. We applaud those Christians who reject this teaching of contempt, and we do not blame them for the sins committed by their ancestors" (National Jewish Scholars Project, "*Dabru Emet*," July 15, 2002, http://www.jcrelations.net/Dabru_Emet_-_A_Jewish_Statement_on_Christians_and_Christianity.2395.0.html).

15. I honestly had never heard the names of Barton Stone or Alexander Campbell (the founders of our movement) until I became a Presbyterian as an adult. Many church historians neglect the Restoration Movement because churches in the Stone-Campbell movement generally do not invest educational resources or time in their own history.

16. Some would argue this point forcefully. See Uwe Siemon-Netto, *The Fabricated Luther: Refuting Nazi Connections and Other Modern Myths*, 2nd ed. (St. Louis: Concordia, 2007).

17. David Nirenberg writes, "Luther launched an armada of arguments whose force led to the acceptance of his way of reading [Scripture] by many and its violent rejection by many more. It was the active prosecution of this conflict of ideas that reshaped the ways in which European Christians experienced their world, and heightened the dangerous significance of Jews and Judaism in that world" (David Nirenberg, *Anti-Judaism: The Western Tradition* [New York: Norton], 256). Also: "Luther's reconceptualization of the ways in which language mediates between God and creation was achieved by thinking with, about, and against Jews and Judaism. Insofar as these reconfigurations diminished the utility and heightened the dangers Jews posed to the Christian world, they had the potential to transform figures of Judaism and their fates. How powerful this potential might be, and what work it might perform in the future, were not Luther's to control" (267). Nirenberg rightly draws a connection between Luther's (hermeneutic toward the) reading of Scripture and the foil he creates in Judaism. To his credit, Nirenberg also avoids a simplistic distinction between the so-called "early Luther" and the "later Luther." Helpfully, he begins by examining Luther's anti-Jewish work on the Psalms, a work representing the so-called "early Luther."

18. Martin Luther, *On the Jews and Their Lies* (1543; repr., East Sussex: Historical Review Press, 2011), 1.

19. Elie Wiesel, *Night*, trans. Stella Rodway (1958; repr., New York: Penguin, 1981), 13.

20. Luther, *The Jews and Their Lies*, 111.

21. Wiesel, *Night*, 19.

22. Luther, *The Jews and Their Lies*, 111.

23. Wiesel, *Night*, 99, 100.

24. Luther, *The Jews and Their Lies*, 111.

25. Elie Wiesel, preface to *Night* (New York: Hill and Wang, 2006), viii.

26. Luther, *The Jews and Their Lies*, 111.

27. Wiesel, *Night*, 21.

28. Luther, *The Jews and Their Lies*, 111.

29. Wiesel, *Night*, 19.

30. Luther, *The Jews and Their Lies*, 112.

31. Wiesel, *Night*, 21.

32. Ibid., 86.

33. Luther, *The Jews and Their Lies*, 114.

34. Wiesel, *Night*, 50.

35. Luther, *The Jews and Their Lies*, 31.

36. Ibid., 114.

37. Wiesel, *Night*, 65–66.

38. Luther, *The Jews and Their Lies*, 131.

39. Wiesel, *Night*, 16.

40. Luther, *The Jews and Their Lies*, 116.

41. Evangelical Lutheran Church bishop Martin Sasse (and a member of the Nazi party) republished Luther's *The Jews and Their Lies* soon after *Kristallnacht*. Sasse encouraged Christians to continue what Luther's words envisioned. See Daniel Jonah Goldhagen, *Hitler's Willing Executioners: Ordinary Germans and the Holocaust* (New York: Vintage, 1997), 109.

Chapter 4: On the Border of Dogma and Underdogma

1. I use the phrase "most Christians" here. I truly hope that this is true. At least among the Christians I have met Nazis are considered evil—maybe even the archetype of evil.

2. C. S. Lewis, *Mere Christianity* (New York: Macmillan, 1956), 11. Lewis does not explain what Nazi morality was. But a word of summary might be helpful. Many Nazis adopted a kind of neo-paganism. Here is a short diary entry by a prison chaplain, August Eckardt, who had several conversations with a Nazi named Dr. Werner Braune. According to Eckardt, Dr. Braune believed that "man is the measure of all things. Whatever makes sense to me in my conscience, that which corresponds to my essence [*Wesen*] and appears appropriate to my being [*artgerecht*], must be the divine presence inside of me. From this follows logically that God is also the source of evil because God put the inclination to do evil inside me. Since I am his creature, why would God not want me to be this way?" (Katharina von Kellenbach, *Mark of Cain: Guilt and Denial in the Post-War Lives of Nazi Perpetrators* [Oxford: Oxford Univ. Press, 2013], 66–67). Braune believed that God's nature must follow from the laws of nature, which includes an apparent law of "survival of the fittest." For more on the general motives of German supporters of National Socialism, see Daniel Jonah Goldhagen, *Hitler's Willing Executioners: Ordinary Germans and the Holocaust* (New York: Knopf, 1996).

3. Lewis, preface to *Mere Christianity*, vi.

4. Susannah Heschel, *The Aryan Jesus* (Princeton: Princeton Univ. Press, 2008), 2.

5. From his *The Letter to the Magnesians* 10.3; this is my own translation. The most popular translations of this statement render "Judaizing" as "Judaism." It is important to note that Judaizing in this context refers to those who are not Jewish but act like they are.

6. Peter Longerich, *Heinrich Himmler: A Life* (Oxford: Oxford Univ. Press, 2012), 270.

7. Lewis, *Mere Christianity*, 66.

8. Robert P. Ericksen, *Complicity in the Holocaust: Churches and Universities in Nazi Germany* (Cambridge: Cambridge Univ. Press, 2012), 28.

9. As quoted from Goldhagen, *Hitler's Willing Executioners*, 114. Niemoeller's quote comes from a public lecture he delivered in Zurich in 1946.

10. "Martin Niemoeller," Jewish Virtual Library, https://www.jewishvirtuallibrary.org/jsource/biography/niemoeller.html.

11. Von Kellenbach, *Mark of Cain*, 4.

12. Ibid., 72.

13. Ibid., 71. Another version of Schmidt's statement is preserved in American records. The American version is provided by von Kellenbach, *Mark of Cain*, 233n55.

14. Ibid.

15. Ibid., 72–73.

16. Ibid., 113.

17. Hannah Arendt, *Eichmann in Jerusalem: A Report on the Banality of Evil* (London: Penguin, 2006).

18. C. S. Lewis, "The Inner Ring" (lecture, King's College, Cambridge, UK, 1944); accessed May 2016, http://www.lewissociety.org/innerring.php.

19. Quoted from Walter Hooper, *C. S. Lewis: Complete Guide to His Life and Works* (New York: HarperCollins, 2005), 269.

20. Von Kellenbach, *Mark of Cain,* 74.

21. I am grateful to Amy-Jill Levine for our personal correspondence and for her time here in Dayton at United Theological Seminary and Westminster Presbyterian Church. I am also grateful to Dayton's Ryterband Symposium for making Levine's visit possible.

22. Rabbi Shmuley Boteach, "The Moral Disintegration of Jimmy Carter," *New York Observer*, August 11, 2014, http://observer.com/2014/08/the-moral-disintegration-of-jimmy-carter/.

23. Jimmy Carter, *Through the Year with Jimmy Carter* (Grand Rapids: Zondervan, 2011), 204.

24. Ibid., 142.

25. Ibid., 312.

26. Ibid., 198.

27. Ibid., 145.

28. Lori Grisham, "Jimmy Carter: Jesus Would Approve of Gay Marriage," *Religion News Service*, July 8, 2015, http://www.religionnews.com/2015/07/08/jimmy-carter-jesus-would-approve-of-gay-marriage/.

29. Anthony Le Donne, "Jesus and Jewish Leadership," in *Jesus among Friends and Enemies*, ed. Larry W. Hurtado and Chris Keith (Grand Rapids: Baker Academic, 2011), 199–220.

30. Christopher Wells, "Pope Francis: Rigidity Is a Sign of a Weak Heart," *Vatican Radio*, December 15, 2014, http://en.radiovaticana.va/news/2014/12/15/pope_francis_rigidity_is_a_sign_of_a_weak_heart/1114830.

31. C. S. Lewis, *Reflections on the Psalms* (New York: Harcourt, Brace, and Company, 1958), 66–67. Stanley Rosenbaum argues that Lewis might not have had such a limited view of the Psalms had he been able to read them in Hebrew ("Our Own Silly Faces," accessed November 2015, http://www.religion-online.org/showarticle.asp?title=1684).

Chapter 5: On the Border of Anti-Judaism and Philo-Judaism

1. Michael O. Emerson and Christian Smith, *Divided by Faith: Evangelical Religion and the Problem of Race in America* (Oxford: Oxford Univ. Press, 2000), ix.

2. David Nirenberg, *Anti-Judaism: The Western Tradition* (New York: Norton), 1–2.

3. Ibid., 468.

4. Ted Cohen, *Jokes: Philosophical Thoughts on Joking Matters* (Chicago: Univ. of Chicago Press, 1999), 80.

5. Michael Lerner and Cornel West, *Jews and Blacks: A Dialogue on Race, Religion, and Culture in America* (New York: Plume, 1996), 43.

6. Ibid., 65.

7. Ibid., 64–65.

8. By the way, I love this book by Lerner and West. I wouldn't want to give an overall negative impression. Sometimes dialogue can spotlight our missteps in helpful ways.

9. I recently learned that this stereotype of Jews is widespread in China. I do not know how many Jews are presently living in China, but I imagine that the ratio of Jews to Gentiles in China isn't impressive.

10. Gary Porton, "Jewish and Christian Theology and Relations after the Holocaust," MyJewishLearning.com, July 30, 2003, accessed November 2015, http://www.myjewishlearning.com/article/judaism-and-christianity-after-the-holocaust/.

11. Nirenberg, *Anti-Judaism*, 468.

12. Martin Luther, "That Jesus Christ Was Born a Jew," *Luther's Works*, 45.201.

13. C. S. Lewis, foreword to *Smoke on the Mountain: An Interpretation of the Ten Commandments*, by Joy Davidman (Philadelphia: Westminster, 1953), 7–8.

14. C. S. Lewis, "Letter to Arthur Greeves, (1933)" in *The Quotable Lewis*, ed. Wayne Martindale and Jerry Root (Wheaton, IL: Tyndale, 1989), 347.

15. John Henry Newman, "St. Chrysostom," in *The Newman Reader*, http://www.newmanreader.org/works/historical/volume2/saints/chrysostom/chapter2.html.

16. John Chrysostom, *Homily* 1.2.5–6.

17. Paul Tillich, *Systematic Theology* (Chicago: Univ. of Chicago Press, 1966), 1:12–14.

18. In a recent interview, Rowan Williams said, "Quite a lot of what Lewis writes about in his Narnia books and elsewhere is about this transition from the god who is really just a fairy godmother fulfilling our wishes to a god who is real and therefore can be quite threatening. One of the themes that keeps coming up in the Narnia books is that we can sometimes experience God as threating. Just because he is so different. Just because he is not a mail-order god that we thought about, decided what he ought to do, and then appointed to the office—the vacancy—in our minds and our hearts. And I think that's partly why Lewis, in the Narnia books, gives God the form of a lion." "Why Read C. S. Lewis for Lent?" englewoodreview.org/rowan-williams-on-church-c-s-lewis-dostoevsky-and-more-video/2/; accessed June 17, 2015.

19. Richard L. Rubenstein, *After Auschwitz: Radical Theology and Contemporary Judaism* (Indianapolis: Bobbs-Merrill, 1966), 70–71, emphasis original.

20. Ibid., 71.

21. Ibid.

22. Michael Wyschogrod, *The Body of Faith: God in the People of Israel* (London: Jason Aronson, 1996), 59.

23. Rubenstein, *After Auschwitz*, 71.

24. Ibid.

25. Ibid., 71–72.

26. My thanks to Larry Behrendt for this observation.

Chapter 6: On the Border of Laughter and Intimacy

1. My sister tells me that these were abandoned carpet samples that our mother got for free.

2. C. S. Lewis, "Letters (1956)," *The Quotable Lewis* (ed. Wayne Martindale and Jerry Root; Wheaton: Tyndale, 1989), 347. It is also noteworthy that Lewis's civil union with Joy Davidman took place in 1956.

3. I would never want to imply that Christians are not funny or that they do not think deeply about humor. I will say, however, that in my research on the philosophy of humor, jokes, and laughter, Christian treatments are few and far between. The notable exception might be found in the Italian Renaissance where a single generation of Italians wrote at least eight works on the topic of comedy: Fausto (1511), Robortello (1548), Maggi (1550), Muzio (1551), Scaligero (1561), Trissino (1562), Castelvetro (1570), Da Cagli (1572). All of these authors were influenced by Aristotle's *Poetics,* and most

built explicitly upon that foundation. My favorite in this list is Lodovico Castelvetro who wrote that humor falls into four categories: (1) the slight of a friend; (2) deception of the *naïve*; (3) evil / physical disgrace [related to Aristotle's "ugliness"]; (4) sex. It is noteworthy that Castelvetro wrote about the humorous elements of sex over three hundred years before Freud. See Salvatore Attardo, *Linguistic Theories of Humor, Humor Research 1* (Berlin: Mouton de Gruyter, 1994), 36–42.

4. Perhaps the purest example of verbal humor, to use Cicero's category, is found in the fact that those who use Chinese characters (logograms) with native fluency sometimes enjoy "puns" derived by the shape of the letters rather than the sound of the letters. See Viviane Alleton, *L'écriture chinoise* (Paris: Presses Universitaires de France, 1970), 63–64.

5. Ted Cohen, *Jokes: Philosophical Thoughts on Joking Matters* (Chicago: Univ. of Chicago Press, 1999), 21.

6. This is probably near to what Lodovico Castelvetro (1570) had in mind when he wrote about the humor of slighting one dear to us. Attardo seems to misunderstand this element in Castelvetro when he writes that the slight of a friend "seems to have little to do with humor" (Attardo, *Linguistic Theories*, 42).

7. Lewis encourages lovers to connect through comedy alongside coitus (which he calls Venus): "We must not be totally serious about Venus. Indeed we can't be totally serious without doing violence to our humanity. It is not for nothing that every language and literature in the world is full of jokes about sex. Many of them may be dull or disgusting and nearly all of them are old. But we must insist that they embody an attitude to Venus which in the long run endangers the Christian life far less than a reverential gravity. We must not attempt to find an absolute in the flesh. Banish play and laughter from the bed of love and you may let in a false goddess. She will be even falser than the Aphrodite of the Greeks; for they, even while they worshipped her, knew that she was 'laughter-loving'" (C. S. Lewis, *The Four Loves* [New York: Harcourt, Brace, 1960], 107–8).

8. Cohen, *Jokes*, 29.

9. Ibid., 40.

10. Henri Bergson, excerpt from "Laughter," in *The Philosophy of Laughter and Humor*, ed. John Morreall (Albany: State University of New York Press, 1987), 117–26, here 119.

11. Cohen, *Jokes*, 33.

12. Pew Research Center, "A Portrait of Jewish Americans," October 3, 2013, http://www.pewforum.org/2013/10/01/jewish-american-beliefs-attitudes -culture-survey/.

13. Norman M. Cohen, "A Serious Man," *Journal of Religion and Film* 15.2 (2012): www.unomaha.edu/jrf/Vol15no2/CohenSeriousMan.html.

14. Cohen, *Jokes*, 15.

15. Friedrich Nietzsche, "Thus Spoke Zarathustra," in *The Portable Nietzsche*, ed. and trans. Walter Kaufmann (London: Penguin, 1976), 103–339, here 185.

16. Sarah Blacher Cohen, "Introduction: The Varieties of Jewish Humor," in *Jewish Wry: Essays on Jewish Humor*, ed. S. B. Cohen (Bloomington: Indiana Univ. Press, 1987), 1–15, here 5.

17. Joseph Telushkin, *Jewish Humor: What the Best Jewish Jokes Say about the Jews* (New York: Harper, 1992), 117.

18. Ibid., 109.

19. Ibid., 111.

20. Ibid., 108.

21. Blacher Cohen, "Varieties of Jewish Humor," 5.

22. Comedians in Cars Getting Coffee, accessed November 2015, http:// comediansincarsgettingcoffee.com/single-shots/hitler.

23. Jason Kalman, "Heckling the Divine: Woody Allen, the Book of Job, and Jewish Theology after the Holocaust," in *Jews and Humor*, ed. Leonard Greenspoon (West Lafayette: Perdue Univ. Press, 2011), 189 (emphasis added).

Chapter 7: On the Border of Tolerance and Love

1. Henri J. M. Nouwen, *In the Name of Jesus: Reflections on Christian Leadership* (New York: Crossroad, 1989), 82–84.

2. Michael Wyschogrod passed away as I was writing this chapter. I never had a chance to meet him, but the loss is significant. His was a unique voice in Jewish-Christian dialogue, and it will be missed.

3. Michael Wyschogrod, *The Body of Faith: God in the People of Israel* (London: Jason Aronson, 1996), 60.

4. Compare Jacques Derrida on this point: "It is possible to love more than one person, Aristotle seems to concede; to love in number, but not too much so—not too many. . . . A finite being could not possibly be present *in act* to too great a number. There is no belonging or friendly community that is present, and first present to *itself, in act*, without election and without selection" (Jacques Derrida, *The Politics of Friendship*, trans. George Collins [London: Verso, 1997], 21, emphasis original).

5. Wyschogrod, *Body of Faith*, 61.

6. Josephus, *Antiquities of the Jews* 1.215.

7. Ibid., 4.223.

8. Ibid., 6.58

9. Ibid., 7.154.

10. It helps, of course, if the two parties are of equal social standing so to avoid a power disparity.

11. Percy Bysshe Shelley, "On Love," in *The Prose and Poetry of Europe and America*, ed. G. P. Morris and N. P. Willis (New York: Leavitt and Allen, 1845), 332.

12. C. S. Lewis, *The Four Loves* (New York: Harcourt, Brace, 1960), 133–34.

13. Denis de Rougemont, *Love in the Western World*, trans. Montgomery Belgion (Princeton: Princeton Univ. Press, 1983), 15.

14. For more on ancient Jewish attitudes toward marriage, see my book *The Wife of Jesus: Ancient Texts and Modern Scandals* (London: Oneworld, 2013).

15. Wyschogrod, *Body of Faith*, 63.

16. C. S. Lewis, *The Four Loves*, 175.

17. Wyschogrod, *Body of Faith*, 62.

18. Ibid., 61.

19. Slavoj Žižek, *Enjoy Your Symptom! Jaques Lacan in Hollywood and Out*, rev. ed. (New York: Routledge, 2001), 8.

20. This is not to say that mainliners do not demonstrate such love. Here I mean to show the value of mission without the scruples of tolerance.

21. Derrida writes, "'Love' wants to possess. It wants the possessing. . . . It always hopes for new property; and even the very Christian 'love of one's neighbour'—charity perhaps—would reveal only a new lust of this fundamental drive" (*Politics of Friendship*, 65).

22. Michael Wyschogrod, "Divine Election and Commandments," in *Abraham's Promise: Judaism and Jewish-Christian Relations* (Grand Rapids: Eerdmans, 2004), 27–28.

23. Wyschogrod, *Body of Faith*, 63. He also writes, "In the Bible, it is not Abraham who moves toward God but God who turns toward Abraham with an election that is not explained because it is an act of love that requires no explanation" (64).

24. Ibid., 64. He continues, "[God's anger] is above all jealousy, the jealousy of one deeply in love who is consumed with torment at the knowledge that his beloved seeks the affection of others."

25. For a book-length treatment of this theme, see Terence E. Fretheim, *The Suffering of God: An Old Testament Perspective* (Minneapolis: Fortress, 1984).

26. Jon Levenson, *The Love of God: Divine Gift, Human Gratitude, and Mutual Faithfulness in Judaism* (Princeton: Princeton Univ. Press, 2015), 4.

27. Ibid., 26.

28. Levenson writes, "In the Bible, for the most part, a covenant is a kind of treaty; it establishes or formalizes a relationship and spells out the obligations." The treaty between the Lord and Israel is "a relationship of service founded not in conquest and subjugation but in good relations and mutual benefit" (Ibid., 5–6).

29. Ibid., 9–10.

30. Ibid., 14.

31. Ibid., 17.

32. Ibid., 16. Anecdotally, my personal conversations with Larry Hurtado (New Testament scholar) confirm that the emphasis on divine love for a particular people is not a common feature in Greek or Roman thought. Scholars of the Hellenic and Hellenistic periods are inclined to think that Israel's love covenant is unique when compared to neighboring ideologies.

Conclusion

1. "Ben" kindly read over these paragraphs and provided permission to share his story.

2. Soong-Chan Rah, *The Next Evangelicalism: Freeing the Church from Western Cultural Captivity* (Downers Grove, IL: Intervarsity, 2009), 29. Rah makes "the distinction between the negative impact of an excessive individualism found in Western culture versus the healthy role of individuation. Individuation is a valuable Western philosophical, psychological contribution which allows for the healthy and necessary differentiation of the individual from family/society/culture/people groups/ nations" (31). Evangelicalism, Rah argues, has suffered from excessive individualism. "The priority of the individual shapes how American evangelicals live out our local church experience, how we study and learn Scripture, how we shape our corporate worship and even how we live and interact in community. For example, our Bible studies become the search for a personal and individualized understanding" (33).

3. Michael O. Emerson and Christian Smith, *Divided by Faith: Evangelical Religion and the Problem of Race in America* (Oxford: Oxford Univ. Press, 2000), 77.

4. Howard Schulweis, *For Those Who Can't Believe: Overcoming the Obstacles to Faith* (New York: HarperCollins, 1994), 86.

5. English translations of the Bible that use the word religion would do better with the words tradition or custom.

6. Brent Nongbri, *Before Religion: A History of a Modern Concept* (New Haven: Yale Univ. Press, 2013).

7. Talal Asad, "Reading a Modern Classic: W. C. Smith's *The Meaning and End of Religion,*" *History of Religions* 40 (2001): 205–22.

8. W. C. Smith, *The Meaning and End of Religion: A New Approach to the Religious Traditions of Mankind* (New York: Macmillan, 1963), 61.

9. Steve Mason, *Josephus, Judea, and Christian Origins: Methods and Categories* (Peabody: Hendrickson, 2009), 160.

10. Ibid., 159.

11. Ibid., 160. Daniel Boyarin and N. T. Wright have suggested that something like religion begins to emerge alongside Christian doctrine. Boyarin and Wright (each in their own way) have suggested that the emergence of Christianity *as an abstract system of beliefs* marks a sea change in sacred demarcation. Boyarin suggests that Judaism as an abstract system of ideas emerged in response to Christian anti-Judaism. Tom Wright has recently called Paul the "first Christian theologian," arguing that other Jewish thinkers did not utilize a constellation of abstract ideas in a way that became "load-bearing" for communal identity. Each of these arguments has met controversy. I will not attempt to detail their arguments or align myself with either of them. I will simply point out that representatives from various ideological camps have converged on a similar hypothesis: Christianity represents a categorical shift toward religious abstraction in a world that did not conceive of religion as a discrete area of life. Moreover, the children of Israel coalesce around an abstract system of ideas in response to Christianity. (Daniel Boyarin, *Border Lines: The Partition of Judaeo-Christianity* [Divinations: Rereading Late Ancient Religion; Philadelphia: Univ. of Pennsylvania Press, 2006]; N. T. Wright, "Why and How Paul Invented 'Christian Theology'"; Lecture at Duke Divinity School, Nov. 11, 2014; accessed: December 2015.) Whether we point to the emergence of religion after the European enlightenment or alongside Christian doctrine, speaking of Second Temple Judaism in terms of religion makes us vulnerable to category errors. More to the point, the application of the suffix -ism may mislead us from the start, as such an abstraction is not well attested in the Second Temple period.

12. C. S. Lewis, *Reflections on the Psalms* (New York: Harcourt, Brace, and Company, 1958), 47.

13. The New Testament does give us examples of life-changing theophanies and epiphanies of individuals. But the language of saving or being saved is not normally attached to these stories. Moreover, the New Testament also gives us examples of entire families being baptized through the opening of one person's heart (Acts 16:11–15). It also tells of unbelieving spouses who are sanctified by the belief of their wife or husband (1 Cor. 7:14) and women being "saved through childbearing" (1 Tim. 2:15). These are troubling passages to Christians with individualistic notions of salvation. (Admittedly, I find 1 Timothy troubling for a number of reasons.) I do not claim to know exactly what these authors had in mind as Christianity began to take shape; I will say, however, that being saved seems much more intricately relational and familial than most individualist Christians assume.

14. Not only am I uncomfortable playing this part (I don't think that one should attempt to be a historian and an apologist at the same time), the connection between historical evidence and faith is probably too complex to explain in an email. Or maybe I just have not yet landed on any sort of satisfactory explanation of how faith relates to historical inquiry. My feeling is that if you're looking for an apologist, I am happy to point you to others who play this part more comfortably.

15. Compare C. S. Lewis's position on this point: "My own position is not Fundamentalist, if Fundamentalism means accepting as a point of faith at the outset the proposition 'Every statement in the Bible is completely true in the literal, historical sense.' That would break down at once on the parables. All the same commonsense and general understanding of literary kinds would forbid anyone to take the parables as historical statements. . . . Books like Esther, or Jonah, or Job which deal with otherwise unknown characters living in unspecified period, & pretty well proclaim themselves to be sacred fiction. Such distinctions are not new. Calvin left the historicity of Job an open question and, from earlier, St. Jerome said that the whole Mosaic account of creation was done 'after the method of a popular poet.' Of course I believe the composition, presentation, & selection for the inclusion in the Bible, of all the books to have been guided by the Holy Ghost. But I think He meant us to have sacred myth & sacred fiction as well as sacred history" (C. S. Lewis, "Letter to Janet Wise, 5 Oct. 1955," in *The Collected Letters of C. S. Lewis, Volume III: Narnia, Cambridge, and Joy 1950–1963* [San Francisco: HarperOne, 2007], 652–53).

16. I am grateful to Gloriajean for providing me the transcript of her sermon.

17. Haviva Ner-David, *Life on the Fringes: A Feminist Journey toward Traditional Rabbinic Ordination* (Teaneck, NJ: Ben Yehuda, 2010), 67–68.

18. Ibid., 133.

19. Stendahl's three rules for religious understanding are discussed in Larry Behrendt's "Rules of Order," Jewish-Christian Intersections (blog), http://jewishchristianintersections.com/?page_id=9.

20. Richard L. Rubenstein, *After Auschwitz: Radical Theology and Contemporary Judaism* (Indianapolis: Bobbs-Merrill, 1966), 62.

21. Ibid., 63.

Afterword

1. "Mount Precipice," Jesus Trail, accessed January 2016, http://jesustrail.com/hike-the-jesus-trail/points-of-interest/mount-precipice.

2. "The Mount of Precipice," Nazareth Cultural and Tourism Association, accessed January 2016, http://www.nazarethinfo.org/En/News/86/2177.